EVIDENCE
and
TRANSCENDENCE

EVIDENCE
and
TRANSCENDENCE

*Religious Epistemology and the
God-World Relationship*

ANNE E. INMAN

University of Notre Dame Press
Notre Dame, Indiana

Copyright © 2008 by University of Notre Dame
Notre Dame, Indiana 46556
www.undpress.nd.edu
All Rights Reserved

Library of Congress Cataloging-in-Publication Data

Inman, Anne E.
Evidence and transcendence : religious epistemology and the God-world relationship / Anne E. Inman.
    p.   cm.
Revision of the author's thesis (doctoral)—Heythrop College.
Includes bibliographical references (p.   ) and index.
ISBN-13: 978-0-268-03177-0 (pbk.)
ISBN-10: 0-268-03177-0 (pbk.)
1. Knowledge, Theory of (Religion)   2. Apologetics.   I. Title.
BL51.I625   2008
212—dc22
                              2008007786

TO DAVID,
my husband

CONTENTS

Acknowledgments	ix
Introduction: Current Challenges	1
Chapter 1. Swinburne and Rationalism	3
Chapter 2. Postliberalism and Lindbeck	35
Chapter 3. The Anti-foundationalism of Thiemann	49
Chapter 4. Schleiermacher and Absolute Dependence	87
Chapter 5. Rahner's "God"	117
Chapter 6. An Alternative Approach	139
Notes	157
Select Bibliography	173
Index	179

ACKNOWLEDGMENTS

With very great pleasure I record my thanks to Philip Endean, my doctoral supervisor, for teaching me so much, for his care and kindness, and for always being at the end of an e-mail in no matter what part of the world. My examiner, Janet Martin Soskice, provided invaluable advice for the revision of the dissertation into its present form, as did an anonymous reader for the University of Notre Dame Press. I am also grateful to Michael Kirwan and Anna Abram, who were doctoral students with me at Heythrop College in the University of London, for their friendship and encouragement then and now. When the task I had set myself seemed overwhelming, I received very necessary encouragement from Laurence Hemming, Dean of Research Students; my thanks go to him and to all the staff at Heythrop College for their help and kindness over the years.

Without the unfailing support of David, my husband, this work would not have been possible at all. This book is dedicated to him. My thanks also go to our sons, Ben and Tom, who, by simply being there, have made their own invaluable contribution.

Introduction

Current Challenges

Over the last four centuries difficult questions have arisen in the area of religious epistemology. Christian apologetics faces two major challenges: the classic Enlightenment insistence on the need to provide evidence for anything that is put forward for belief; and the argument that all human knowledge is mediated by finite reality and thus "knowledge" of a being interpreted as completely other than finite reality is impossible or meaningless. Christian apologists have tended to understand their task primarily, if not exclusively, in terms of one of these challenges. The philosopher Richard Swinburne, for example, mounts a defense of Christianity by making claims about the evidence for its teachings, supported by probability theory. The theologian Ronald Thiemann, by contrast, aims to defend the Christian doctrine of revelation without committing the epistemological faults that the second challenge has exposed. God cannot be known in the same way that a finite object is known, but on the other hand, Thiemann claims, knowing God cannot be a knowing that is cut off from ordinary philosophical epistemology.

This work sets out to demonstrate that neither kind of response, as exemplified in the thought of Swinburne and Thiemann, is satisfactory. George Lindbeck is also included in the discussion here, with Thiemann. Like Thiemann, he addresses the challenge posed by the mediation of knowledge, but he differs from Thiemann in that he sees no need to defend Christian doctrine, rejecting altogether the need for any justification of faith. Neither Swinburne nor Thiemann (as well as Lindbeck) is able to uphold the notion of God's "transcendence" or absolute otherness; neither is able to articulate a sound account of how the human being can be said to know God, or even to articulate a sound account of how the human being can know anything at all. This study will further show that both approaches rely on an unsatisfactory account of human freedom. In addition, Swinburne ignores the legitimate concerns behind the second challenge, and Thiemann (largely) and Lindbeck ignore those behind the first.

Why the failure of these responses? What we discover, I argue, is an inadequate philosophy of God. Neither Swinburne nor Thiemann and Lindbeck include in their philosophical theology the notion of God as first cause of existence itself—namely, as the ultimate cause of all that is. In this omission they follow the general trend of Christian apologetics in the seventeenth and eighteenth centuries, as analyzed so originally by Michael J. Buckley in his *At the Origins of Modern Atheism*. Following from the failure to recognize God as first cause is a failure to understand the proper relationship between God and the world. This in turn results in a deficient account of God and a deficient account of the human being. God is portrayed, not only by Swinburne, but also by Thiemann and Lindbeck, as proportionate to, rather than other than, the finite; the human being, cut loose from its ground, is portrayed as the center of existence.

This book is written in the belief that it is possible for Christian apologetics to do justice to both these challenges: the need for evidence and the insistence on the mediation of knowledge. Not only is this apologetic task possible; it is crucially necessary for the contemporary defense of Christian faith. Painstaking work is required to clarify the philosophical understanding both of God's transcendence and of God's knowability. The effort will reap surplus rewards by uncovering a sound account of human knowing and of human freedom—indeed, of human being itself.

An exploration of the theologies of Karl Rahner and Friedrich Schleiermacher provides material for the constructive work in this book. Their theologies, though in many respects mutually incompatible, nonetheless exhibit surprising similarities in matters pertaining to religious epistemology. And, as will become apparent, their shared thinking in this respect offers an alternative to the kinds of approaches represented by Swinburne's rationalism and the postliberalism of Theimann and Lindbeck.

CHAPTER 1
Swinburne and Rationalism

The philosopher Richard Swinburne is acutely conscious of the threat to religious belief, in particular Christian belief, posed by the argument that any truth claim must be justified or grounded in evidence. Dismissing the appeal to faith alone, he accepts the need to provide justification for Christian beliefs. Accordingly, he attempts to reassert the role of the metaphysical in religious epistemology by what he considers rational, even "scientific," argument. The three elements of Swinburne's defense of Christian faith are laid out in his trilogy: in *The Coherence of Theism*[1] he asserts the meaningfulness and coherence of the claim that there is a God; in *The Existence of God*[2] he sets out his empirical argument for the probable existence of God; and in *Faith and Reason*[3] he argues that the specific beliefs of the Christian Church are more probable than any religious alternative. When these works first appeared in the 1970s and 1980s they were ambitious attempts to meet, on their own terms, twentieth-century philosophical critics who rejected religious belief as irrational or unjustified.

Swinburne does not argue explicitly that God exists. He argues, rather, that theism is coherent and that belief in God is not unscientific and not irrational. He sets out to prove that there are good a posteriori arguments—arguments from evidence—that make it probable that God exists. These arguments will be inductive, not analytic; they will have the power not merely to expound and justify but to persuade. Swinburne claims that it is possible, by force of rational argument, to demonstrate not merely that holding a theistic belief is as rational as holding no such belief, but also that logically one should embrace theism rather than atheism. This same process, he claims, may be used to prove that logically one should opt for Christianity rather than any theistic alternative.

But how satisfactory, from an epistemological viewpoint, is Swinburne's defense of the coherence of theism and the probable existence of God? And from a philosophical and theological perspective, how well does it uphold the notion of God's transcendence? To answer these questions, it is necessary to examine in detail Swinburne's religious epistemology and his philosophy of God. It will also be pertinent to consider just how well his account of Christian faith resonates with standard Christian teachings.

The Defense of the Coherence of Theism

In arguing the case for theism, Swinburne defines the theist as someone who holds certain core beliefs common to all theists, for example, that God is perfectly good and knows everything. In addition to these core beliefs, the theist may or may not hold further beliefs:

> By a theist I understand a man who believes that there is a God. By a 'God' he understands something like a 'person without a body (i.e. a spirit) who is eternal, free, able to do anything, knows everything, is perfectly good, is the proper object of human worship and obedience, the creator and sustainer of the universe'. Christians, Jews, and Muslims are all in the above sense theists. Many theists also hold further beliefs about God, and in these Christians, Jews, and Muslims differ among themselves; and yet further beliefs, in which some members of each group differ from others. Christians assert, and Jews and Muslims deny, that God became incarnate in Jesus Christ. Roman Catholics assert, and Protestants deny, that Christ is 'really' present in the bread consecrated in the Mass.[4]

Swinburne's definition of a theist occurs at the start of *The Coherence of Theism*, the first volume of his trilogy on philosophical theology, and his subsequent theological considerations presuppose this understanding of theism. He takes as his premise that a Christian or a Jew or a Muslim has a core set of beliefs about God, which includes such things as God's perfection, and also has other beliefs that make him or her specifically a Christian or a Jewish or a Muslim theist. Swinburne proposes a philosophical inquiry that takes the core beliefs as primary: those beliefs not held in common are "further" or secondary beliefs.

It is instructive to note here that in *Faith and Reason*, the final volume of his trilogy, Swinburne examines the role of creeds in religious faith and claims that it is the creed of a particular religion that articulates the secondary beliefs, and that by examining the different creeds one may compare the different theological systems. He thus suggests that one may, as it were, stand outside the different approaches to faith and choose between them. The rational person can examine evidence relating to different faith systems and decide which is more likely to satisfy him or her: the belief which someone needs in order to pursue a religious way is "the belief that pursuit of his way is more likely to attain his goals than is pursuit of any other way."[5] In the relationship between God and the human being, the initiative seems to be clearly with the human being. The image evoked is that of a person presented with an array of religious ideas and the responsibility to choose between them. In assessing Swinburne's theism, it will be important to ask whether this image is compatible with a religious outlook in general and with standard Christian teachings in particular.

When Swinburne, who has developed his philosophy of religion in a profoundly atheistic philosophical environment, seeks to defend the meaningfulness, that is to say the coherence, of theism, he intentionally makes use of the very tools of the analytic philosophy that was being newly developed at Oxford and that virtually ruled out the possibility of religious belief. Analytic philosophy, in the shape of the logical positivism represented by A. J. Ayer, had pushed to the extreme the post-Enlightenment requirement for evidence as a precondition for any form of intellectual assent. According to logical positivism, any statement that could not be verified was meaningless.[6] Its arguments persuaded many philosophers, most notably J. L. Austin, that the philosophical task consisted in teaching what words mean in ordinary usage so that meaningless philosophical theses could be avoided. This aim is characteristic of ordinary-language philosophy, another form of analytic philosophy.

Swinburne, however, is neither an ordinary-language philosopher nor one prepared to absolve religious belief from the requirement for evidence. On the contrary, he intends to supply evidence in support of the rationality of religious belief using the very theories of verification that purported to herald the collapse of religion among thinking people. He also attempts to rework those same theories to construct a metaphysical theological system within the Western, Christian tradition of metaphysics. On the prevailing philosophical view, this tradition has been thoroughly discredited. Yet as Christian faith comes under attack because it seems unable to provide evidence in support of its claims, Swinburne maintains that the credibility of metaphysics can be restored.

Swinburne calls on the findings of modern science, usually considered a threat to religious belief, and uses what he terms a "scientific" method to build his metaphysical system. On the face of it, he concedes, Christian faith cannot be justified because God is beyond observation, and therefore God's existence cannot be verified. Yet, Swinburne argues, much of modern science would be rendered meaningless if, for a theory to be meaningful, it must be conclusively verifiable by observation. He claims that there are innumerable scientific facts that are beyond observation and yet verifiable. And the same holds for facts about God. For Swinburne, it is possible to demonstrate how facts about God may be verified through the reestablishment of a metaphysical system. Swinburne draws on three sources in establishing a metaphysics for the defense of theism: analytic philosophy, scientific discovery, and the metaphysics of premodern thought.

The Appeal to the Meaning of Language

In response to those who contend that a statement is meaningless if it cannot be verified or if it attempts to use words outside the meanings conferred by ordinary usage, Swinburne offers a comparison between talk about science and talk about God. The sort of science that he particularly has in mind is the physics of relativity theory and quantum theory, together with the study of the meaning and justification of scientific theories. According to Swinburne, science and religion are comparable in that they both refer to matters that are beyond observation, and thus talk about science and talk about God are on a similar footing.

In his "Intellectual Biography," Swinburne discusses the type of language that should be used for metaphysical issues. "Metaphysical language must take off from and be explained in terms of ordinary language." He acknowledges that "ordinary-language philosophy, in fact, had no sympathy for anything which went beyond ordinary language."[7] (That the word "God" belongs to ordinary language he seems not to have noticed.) Yet he argues that one can use the same type of language—metaphorical, analogous, and so on—for discussion about God as one can use in non-religious contexts. Although J. L. Austin himself had no sympathy with metaphysics, Swinburne adapts what he has learned from Austin to construct a metaphysical system.

Swinburne argues that language can meaningfully refer in situations where verification is not possible and contends that statements about God are meaningful, not because they can be verified, but because they are "analogous." He consciously develops the appeal to "analogy" using Thomas Aquinas, but in a way quite different from the standard interpretation, commenting, "not everyone will agree with my interpretation of Aquinas."[8] Swinburne is unimpressed by Thomas's "emphatic" assertion that we do not and cannot use terms univocally of God and creatures:

> His reasons for this view of are of motley kind, which it would not be useful to discuss in detail, but underlying them seems the basic reason that the 'wisdom', 'goodness', etc. attributed to God are very different from 'wisdom', 'goodness', etc. attributed to men. So he would seem to argue that when we say that God is 'wise' and Socrates is 'wise' we must be using 'wise' in somewhat different senses. For example, he gives as a reason for 'wise' not being univocal when applied to God and man that in a man his wisdom is 'distinct from his essence, power, or existence' whereas in God this distinction does not exist.

Having dismissed Thomas's assertion that we cannot use terms univocally of God and creatures, Swinburne now interprets Thomas as saying the reverse, that we *can* use terms univocally of God and of creatures. "But . . . the fact that 'wisdom' amounts to something very different in God from what it amounts to in men does not show that the term is being used non-univocally—at any rate if 'univocally' means 'in the same sense' in our sense."[9]

In claiming that in Thomas's understanding, "words are used in theology in the same sense . . . as outside," that is to say "univocally," Swinburne dispenses altogether with Thomas's careful distinction between "univocal" and "analogical" when it comes to the use of language for talk about God. In Swinburne's view this distinction is a matter of no consequence. "Nothing of philosophical substance," he claims, "turns on whether my account of Aquinas' doctrine is correct."[10] He could hardly be more mistaken. It is with this distinction that Thomas acknowledges the paradoxical nature of the human claim to "know" God.

Swinburne explains his contention that statements about God are meaningful because they are "analogous" by an appeal to "modern theoretical science—the physics of relativity theory and quantum theory, the biology of evolution, the genetics of DNA—which many people supposed to count against the traditional Christian world-view."[11] What he terms "analogous" language, he argues, is commonly used in science to describe matters that are beyond our observation. Atoms, electrons, and quarks are far too small to be observed in any literal sense, yet may be spoken of "analogically." "What makes scientific theories *meaningful* is not their verifiability, but the fact that they describe their entities (atoms) and their properties (velocity, spin) with words used somewhat similarly to words used for describing ordinary mundane things. Thus atoms are somewhat like billiard-balls, only very much smaller; they are also somewhat like waves, only not waves in media like water."[12] Swinburne concludes that "analogous" language may be used in discussion about God with the same right as it is used in scientific theories and will be similarly meaningful.

Here we come up against the crucial difference between Swinburne's interpretation of "analogy" and Thomas's interpretation, when "analogy" is applied to what is said about God. In Swinburne's view, statements about God function similarly to statements about the scientific world. Just as the operation of an atom may be described in the language used to describe the operation of billiard balls, so the workings of God may be described using language normally associated with the workings of observable phenomena. What Swinburne calls an analogy is essentially a simile: figurative language that is useful up to a point. What he loses in collapsing Thomas's distinction between univocal and analogical is the notion that God acts and we act in ways that are infinitely distinct, because God and we are infinitely distinct. Swinburne fails to take into account what Thomas understood, namely, that language used to describe the workings of created phenomena can be applied only in an extended sense to God, as the source of the phenomena and their operations

In effect, Swinburne's position implies that God is differentiated from created phenomena in the same way that an atom is differentiated from a billiard ball—simply by being beyond human observation. It is inconsistent with the traditional view that there is a qualitative difference between an atom and God, who is is neither finite nor material. In recognition of this qualitative difference the Fourth Lateran Council of 1215 had declared that "between Creator and creature no similitude can be expressed without implying a greater dissimilitude."[13] Thomas's treatment of language about God is founded on the qualitative difference between Creator and creature. According to Thomas, various truths about God's nature—that God is eternal, unchanging, immaterial, and simple (without parts)—can be proved, but these truths are all essentially negative.[14] They set out what God is *not* like without giving any positive insight into God's nature. Analogical language, however, may be used to make positive statements about God through the attribution of perfections. This is possible because those perfections which are present in human beings are derived from God. Thus, "[w]e cannot speak of God at all except on the basis of creatures, and so whatever is said both of God and creatures is said in virtue of a certain order that creatures have in relation to God (*ordo creaturae ad Deum*) as their source and cause in which all their perfections exist."[15]

Nevertheless, for Thomas, words used to attribute perfections to God are not used in the same sense as they are used in relation to the creature. "It is impossible to predicate anything univocally of God and creatures. The reason for this is that every effect which is less than its cause does not represent it adequately, in that the effect is thus not the same sort of thing as the cause. So what exists in a variety of divided forms in the effects exists simply and in a unified way in the cause."[16] So, for example, while perfect goodness may be predicated of God, this does not signify that we have an adequate positive understanding of what perfect goodness means. Nevertheless, because of our relation to God as the source of human goodness, we are saying something meaningful and true when we attribute goodness to God, and we gain some insight into the nature of God. Swinburne's "scientific" treatment of God, in stark contrast, lacks an understanding that this insight into God's nature is something quite different from the insight that one may gain into the nature of a created being.

On Thomas's understanding, our insight regarding God relies on the recognition that there is in the human being a perfection which has God as its source. Thus, for Thomas the human being is the creature who receives perfections from the source of perfection and thereby receives insight about that source from that source. Swinburne's argument implies that we understand God through the resources of our own intellect and thus that the human intellect, rather than God, is the source of knowledge of reality. My concern here is one that will be developed in the course of this study: when Swinburne depicts the human subject at the controlling center of the act of knowing, there is a corresponding loss of the notion of God's transcendence. This is not all, however. For Thomas, God, as the source of perfections, is the source of truth. God as Truth grounds or justifies *all* human knowing, not merely knowledge of God's self. God is the guarantee that human knowledge is reliable. When Swinburne moves the controlling center of the act of knowing to the human being, I would argue, he is then left with no way of demonstrating how any human knowing is grounded. This argument will also be developed as this study proceeds.

Metaphysics in Relation to Science

Swinburne also draws on contemporary science in his defense of religious belief. In his book *Is There a God?*, for example, which relies heavily on material from *The Existence of God,* Swinburne discusses the scientific theories of biologist Richard Dawkins and physicist Stephen Hawking.[17] Both argue on the basis of their scientific theories that there is no God who sustains the world. Swinburne challenges not their scientific theories but their conclusion and argues that the same theories point rather to the opposite conclusion.[18]

In his general approach to contemporary science, Swinburne claims to be following in the footsteps of Thomas Aquinas:

> It was at this time that I discovered that someone else had the programme to use the best science and philosophy of his day to rigorously establish Christian theology. I read Part I of the *Summa Theologiae* of Thomas Aquinas. He too started from where the secular world was in his day—the thirteenth century—and used the best secular philosophy available, that of Aristotle, instead of the initially more Christian-looking philosophy of Plato; and he sought to show that reflection on the observable world, as described by Aristotelian science, led inescapably to its creator, God.[19]

Thomas's purposes, however, were very different from Swinburne's. Thomas was untroubled by Swinburne's primary concern: the need to provide evidence for those things put forward for belief. The *Summa Theologiae*, with its famous Five Ways, was written for the benefit of Catholic students of theology rather than for unbelievers. Thomas's aim was not to "establish Christian theology" but to explore—to understand and expound—the doctrines that he and they already believed. In contrast, Thomas's *Summa contra Gentiles*, which in many of its articles had covered the same ground as Part I of the *Summa Theologiae*, was written for use by missionaries among Jews and Muslims. Yet even in the *Summa contra Gentiles* Thomas did not regard his scientific and philosophical arguments as grounds for conversion. Rather, his aim was to set out those truths about God and creation that could be established by reasoning and those truths that could be known only by an appeal to divine authority. Conversion to Christianity for the Jews and Muslims of the thirteenth century was a matter of submitting to divine authority in disputed matters such as the doctrine of the Trinity—divine authority that came through the Bible and the teaching of the Christian Church. Swinburne's purposes are quite different.

Against Dawkins and Hawking, Swinburne argues that the view that God sustains the world in turn explains the most up-to-date findings of contemporary science:

> The basic structure of my argument is this. Scientists, historians, and detectives observe data and proceed thence to some theory about what best explains the occurrence of these data. We can analyse the criteria which they use in reaching a conclusion that a certain theory is better supported by the data than a different theory—that is, is more likely, on the basis of those data, to be true. Using those same criteria, we find that the view that there is a God explains *everything* we observe, not just some narrow range of data. It explains the fact that there is a universe at all, that scientific laws operate within it, that it contains conscious animals and humans with very complex intricately organized bodies, that we have abundant opportunities for developing ourselves and the world, as well as the more particular data that humans report miracles and have religious experiences. In so far as scientific causes and laws explain some of these things (and in part they do), these very causes and laws need explaining, and God's action explains them. The very same criteria which scientists use to reach their own theories lead us to move beyond those theories to a creator God who sustains everything in existence.[20]

Thus the existence of God, for Swinburne, explains particular facts of general experience: "[d]esks and trees, stars and galaxies, atoms and electrons,"[21] or "why a ball dropped from a tower 64 feet above the ground takes two seconds to reach the ground."[22] It explains the world and its order.[23]

It is evident that what Swinburne means when he says that his method is "scientific" is that he submits theological questions to the same procedures that are used in science when science deals with matters beyond direct human observation. For Swinburne, traditional metaphysical theories are a type of "higher level" scientific theory. Swinburne states that "scientific theories (or hypotheses) are *justified* insofar as (1) they lead us to expect the phenomena we observe around us; (2) those phenomena are such as we would otherwise not expect to find; and (3) the theories are simple theories."[24] Christian theology, like natural science, is concerned with phenomena and the meaning and justification of the theories that explain these phenomena. What differentiates theories is the level at which the theory operates, and that depends upon the level of the explanation that is sought.

Scientific theories themselves operate at different levels of explanation. And, according to Swinburne, metaphysical theories operate at the highest possible level. Thus a metaphysical theory is a scientific theory, although on a different level than a theory that explains the laws of the physical universe. As Swinburne states in his "Intellectual Biography,"

> Scientific theories each seek to explain a certain limited class of data: Kepler's laws sought to explain the motions of the planets; natural selection seeks to explain the fossil record and various present features of animals and plants. But some scientific theories are higher-level than others, and seek to explain the operation of the lower-level theories and the existence in the first place of the objects with which they deal. Newton's laws explained why Kepler's laws operated; and chemistry has sought to explain why there existed primitive animals and plants in the first place. A metaphysical theory is a highest-level-of-all theory. It seeks to explain why there is a universe at all, why it has the most general laws of nature that it does, and especially such laws as lead to the evolution of animals and humans, as well as any particular phenomena which lower-level laws are unable to explain. Such a theory is meaningful if it can be stated in ordinary words, stretched a bit in meaning perhaps. And it is justified if it is a simple theory and leads you to expect the observable phenomena, when you would not otherwise expect them.[25]

A metaphysical theory is the "highest-level-of-all theory."

Christian theology for Swinburne is thus an explanatory theory (albeit a high-level theory) about what can be observed. But is Swinburne's claim to provide an "ultimate" explanation supported by anything so far? Or does he merely postulate a "God of the gaps," thereby adopting a line of retreat that restricts God's explanatory role to whatever has not yet been explained by current science? Since Swinburne claims to be following the same "program" as Thomas, it is reasonable to pursue further the comparison between Swinburne's approach and Thomas's Scholastic approach.

A metaphysical explanation, according to the medieval Scholastic philosophers and theologians, is one that explains "all that is." Thus Scholasticism would have approved Swinburne's initial distinction between a scientific theory, which seeks to explain a certain limited class of data, and a metaphysical theory, which seeks to explain why there is a universe at all. However, when Swinburne claims that a metaphysical theory seeks to explain why the universe has the laws of nature that it does, he has already blurred this distinction, because the laws of nature are themselves "a certain limited class of data." The confusion is compounded when he claims that a metaphysical theory seeks to explain any particular phenomena that lower-level laws are unable to explain. Here, in fact, is a classic case of a "God of the gaps": Swinburne postulates God as that which explains what science does not explain.

Elsewhere, Swinburne is clearly alert to the danger of merely postulating a "God of the gaps." In his own view, he is "postulating a God" not to explain what science does not explain, but "to explain what science explains."[26] Thus he claims that "any metaphysical theory, such as a Christian theological system, is a higher-level explanatory theory" that explains observable phenomena. One has only to turn to the Darwinian theory of evolution by natural selection, according to Swinburne, to recognize the need for a higher-level theory. Darwin's theory is able to provide an explanation of the evolution of human and animal bodies but not an ultimate explanation. "[O]ur problem is to explain why some physical state caused the emergence of souls with such mental properties as beliefs, desires, purposes, thoughts and sensations. Darwinism is of no use in solving this problem. . . . But theism can provide an explanation of these things. God being omnipotent, is able to join souls to bodies. . . . He has good reason to cause the existence of souls and join them to bodies."[27]

Thus theology functions in the same way as a scientific hypothesis, differing only in being a "highest-level hypothesis." Darwin's theory can explain why the human being evolved from the animal, but only a metaphysical or theological theory can explain why the soul should be joined to the human body. For Swinburne, "ultimate explanation" and "highest-level hypothesis" are one and the same.

The "soul" example makes particularly clear that God, for Swinburne, is the explanation for one thing rather than another, for a "this" rather than a "that." Thus, theism and the theory of evolution each deal with different aspects of evolution. Darwinism explains why one animal develops from another, and theism explains why the human animal acquires a soul. Darwinism explains biological development, while theism explains spiritual development. Swinburne justifies this approach on the grounds that the latter is a higher form of explanation, but, crucially, the higher form of explanation is not qualitatively different from the lower form. Even if one were to grant that spiritual development is a superior form of development and on that basis call the explanation supplied by theism a higher, or even the highest, form of explanation, the theistic explanation is no more *unlike* the Darwinian explanation than the scientific observation of an atom is *unlike* the scientific observation of a billiard ball. God is still understood as one source of explanation *alongside* others. The billiard ball, the atom, and God represent three points on a continuum of the range of things that are known by the knowing subject.

Swinburne's higher form of explanation is not qualitatively different from the lower forms precisely because, like a theory of evolution, it is concerned with certain things that are, as distinct from being concerned with all that is. God is the explanation for souls being joined to bodies, the laws of gravity, desks and trees, stars and galaxies—all observable phenomena, in fact. These phenomena are taken individually, for Swinburne, and each provides further evidence for the argument that God sustains the world. Even if this were not the case, that is, even if Swinburne were considering "all observable phenomena" as a single class or entity, it would still represent a certain class of data since even all observable phenomena cannot necessarily be equated with all that is. And the claim that one can explain all observable phenomena as evidence of a God who sustains those phenomena is problematic: when one posits the explanation for certain things that are, whether they are taken individually or as a class, the explanation is always proportionate to, that is, limited by, those things that are explained. For every phenomenon, for every individual thing, and for every class of data, there is a proportionate explanation. God and nature are thus part of a system that functions together to form the one whole, which consists of all that is.

The result is that the God posited by Swinburne does not transcend the finite world but has been reduced to one factor among others that account for the phenomena of human experience. In the traditional sense of "ultimate explanation," Swinburne's God is not an ultimate explanation.

The Appeal to Traditional Proofs

Swinburne's third main source on which he draws for his defense of theism is the attempt to prove the existence of God characteristic of medieval Christian metaphysics. In preparing for his own defense of the probability that God exists, Swinburne gives considerable attention to the classical arguments for the existence of God: Anselm of Canterbury's ontological argument and Thomas's Five Ways. (It is worth reiterating that Thomas himself was not concerned with providing evidence for the existence of God as a prerequisite for belief. And it was Anselm, of course, who coined the phrase "*fides quaerens intellectum*" or "faith in search of understanding" and gave it as the title to his *Proslogion*, a work "written . . . from the point of view of one trying to raise his mind to contemplate God and seeking to understand what he believes.")[28] It will also be essential to examine Swinburne's view of religious experience and the crucial role it plays in tipping the weight of available evidence in favor of God's probable existence.

In *The Existence of God,* Swinburne considers whether any of the traditional arguments for the existence of God, taken separately or together, are good deductive arguments or good inductive arguments. He immediately dismisses the usefulness of a priori deductive arguments. These are "arguments in which the premisses are conceptual truths, viz. propositions which would be true whether or not there was a universe of material or spiritual beings other than God."[29] Since the premises are a priori, they cannot be empirically verified. They cannot be treated like the findings of natural science. Swinburne includes the ontological argument in this category.

Swinburne also maintains that none of the a posteriori classical arguments for the existence of God make good deductive arguments, since the premises from which they start are far from generally accepted. A strictly deductive or analytic argument could provide a conclusion that would be certain, in the sense that to deny the conclusion would be to contradict the premises. However, the conclusion would only be as persuasive as the premises—and clearly Swinburne is of the opinion that in the classical arguments for the existence of God, the premises, whether they be a priori or a posteriori, are questionable.

Swinburne thus turns to inductive arguments and to conclusions that are less than certain. He aims to supply a posteriori arguments, based on "scientific" findings, "in which the premisses report what are (in some very general sense) features of human experience."[30] The perceived advantage of this approach is that the premises will be verifiable, although the conclusions will not have the certainty of analytic argument since the method is inductive. Swinburne's aim is not to convince beyond a doubt but rather to persuade the rational person, even one with no religious experience, of the probability that God exists.

Specifically, Swinburne claims he can establish that the probability that God exists is greater than one-half. He sees virtue in the fact that the evidence does not provide more compelling evidence, since he takes the view that if he were to argue for too high a degree of probability, then acceptance of the argument would necessitate belief in God, and a person's freedom to choose not to believe would be compromised: "If God's existence, justice, and intentions became items of evident common knowledge, then man's freedom would in effect be vastly curtailed."[31] The extraordinariness of this statement should not be lost on the reader. Swinburne seems to imply that human freedom is dependent upon a degree of human nescience.

The a posteriori arguments that Swinburne examines "claim that something which men experience is grounds for believing that there is a God or that there is no God."[32] Examples of such human experience are evident general truths about the world or features of private human experience. Swinburne discusses the classic cosmological argument, two forms of an argument from design (the teleological argument and the argument from providence), the argument from the existence of consciousness, the so-called moral argument, arguments from miracles and revelation, and the argument from religious experience.

In considering these inductive arguments, Swinburne distinguishes what he calls "P-inductive" arguments, in which the premises make the conclusion probable, from weaker "C-inductive" arguments, in which the premises make the conclusion more likely than it would otherwise be.[33] A correct C-inductive argument "confirms" the conclusion in the sense that it adds, if only a little, to the probability of the conclusion. Swinburne maintains that most of the arguments for the existence of God are good C-inductive arguments—that is to say, their premises make it more likely that God exists than that God does not exist. But the crucial issue for Swinburne is not whether any single argument makes it more likely than not that God exists, but whether all the arguments taken together make it probable that God exists. In other words, the crucial question is whether there is overall a good P-inductive argument for the existence of God. And in the final chapter of *The Existence of God,* called "The Balance of Probability," Swinburne weighs all the evidence and concludes that there is.

The evidence that Swinburne brings to his argument is taken from experience in a very general or very broad sense, comprising all mental perceptions or apparent perceptions of that which is, or appears to be, around us. "An experience," as defined by Swinburne, "is a conscious mental going-on."[34] He treats evidence from experience differently depending upon whether it derives from general human experience, that is to say, the "ordinary" experience that is common to human beings, or from "religious experience," which is distinct from ordinary experience and is restricted to certain persons. For Swinburne, "[w]hat makes an experience religious is the way it seems to the subject." General human experience refers to mental perceptions of the world around us, while religious experience, or an experience of God, is "an apparent perception."[35] A "religious experience" is one "which seems (epistemically) to the subject to be an experience of God . . . or some other supernatural thing."[36]

Although religious experience is only "an apparent perception," the person having it will "in the very general sense . . . perceive God." The awareness of God can be considered a perception in a very general sense, "without implying that the awareness is necessarily mediated via the normal senses." Furthermore, it follows from Swinburne's definition of "perceive" that the experience of God is not the only perception of an object that may occur without the mediation of the senses: he defines it as "the general verb for awareness of something apart from oneself, which may be mediated by any of the ordinary senses—e.g. it may be a matter of seeing or hearing or tasting—or by none of these."[37]

It is plain from the above that Swinburne rejects the challenge to Christian faith implicit in the recognition that all human knowledge, including knowledge of God, is mediated by finite reality. Swinburne does not claim that the apparent perception of God that occurs in the religious experience *is* mediated by the senses. Indeed, for Swinburne, conscious mental goings-on generally may or may not be mediated by the senses.

Swinburne treats evidence differently, depending upon whether it is evidence from general human experience or from religious experience. To the evidence from general human experience, Swinburne applies Bayes's theorem, a mathematical formula used for calculating probabilities. Bayes's theorem is the basic theorem of confirmation theory. It is thus a weak form of verification since it "confirms" a conclusion, in the sense used above: it adds to the probability of a conclusion rather than being conclusive in itself. It provides a C-inductive argument but not a P-inductive argument. The probabilities calculated by Bayes's theorem are "conditional," that is, they relate to specific evidence rather than being a priori. If the galaxies of the heavens suggest an ordered universe, for example, then this piece of evidence moves the balance of probability in favor of the existence of God, since the existence of God would explain the ordering of the universe. The weight added to the probability that God exists is conditional upon the specific evidence for the order of the universe.

When it comes to assessing the evidence of religious experience, however, Swinburne does not employ Bayes's theorem. He grants that religious experience cannot be verified "scientifically." Once again he appeals to an analogy, claiming that the verification of religious experiences is "analogous" to the verification of sense experiences. To evidence taken from religious experience Swinburne applies the "principle of credulity," namely, that apparent perceptions ought to be taken at their face value in the absence of positive reason for challenge.[38] Simply put, we trust our sense experiences unless we have some good reason for not trusting them. The same principle, he argues, should apply to religious experiences.

This type of analogical argument is often contested; C. B. Martin, for example, asserts that "there are no tests agreed upon to establish genuine experience of God and distinguish it decisively from the ungenuine."[39] On the other hand, John Hick and Keith Yandell, like Swinburne, "argue that just as perceptual experience justifies our beliefs about the material world around us, religious experiences warrant beliefs about the divine or sacred."[40] Furthermore, William Alston, Gary Gutting, and William Wainwright use a version of the analogical argument that requires that the tests for religious and sense experience be of a similar nature.[41]

The justification provided by the principle of credulity is evidently circular. Since an experience seems to be an experience of God, then provided there is no evidence to the contrary, it can be taken to be an experience of God. Supporters of this type of justification would say that if we are willing to accept a circular justification in the case of sense experiences, we should be willing to accept such a justification in the case of religious experiences. Swinburne, therefore, regards the fact that many witnesses have testified to an experience of God or to a religious experience as a crucial piece of evidence for the existence of God.

A vital step in Swinburne's overall assessment of the probability of God's existence is that of weighing as a whole all possible evidence for the existence of God. Confirmation theory is concerned with the increase of probability. Swinburne's approach is to look separately at the increase of probability that each piece of evidence brings and then bring all the evidence together for a final assessment. The cumulative effect of evidence is central. Swinburne finds it regrettable that in the philosophy of religion, arguments for the existence of God tend to be treated in isolation from each other. Rather, all evidence must be taken together so that the balance of probability may be weighed. Swinburne's final conclusion, therefore, is that taking into account all the evidence that is available, the truth claims of theism are more probable than not. In reaching this conclusion he takes into account the bulk of the evidence, which has demonstrated C-inductive arguments for God's existence—arguments that make God's existence more likely than it would otherwise be—and the final piece of evidence from religious experience, based on the principle of credulity.

Swinburne's moves here deserve further attention. On the basis of the principle of credulity Swinburne argues that for a person who has had what seems to be an experience of God, the evidence of this religious experience is sufficient to make theism overall probable, unless the probability of theism on other evidence is very low indeed. Even if the probability on other evidence is very low indeed, the testimony of other witnesses who also claim religious experience suffices to make theism overall probable, unless, on other evidence, it is highly improbable. A person who has not had what seems to be an experience of God will have less evidence for the existence of God, "but not very much less, for he will have testimony of many who have had such experiences."[42] Swinburne argues that he has shown that the existence of God is not already on other evidence very improbable, and therefore concludes that the testimony of many witnesses to experiences apparently of God makes the existence of God probable.

It is important to note the considerable weight that Swinburne places on the evidence from religious experience. He deals with religious experience in the penultimate chapter of *The Existence of God*. His conclusion with regard to the evidence up to that point, excluding religious experience, is relatively weak. The validity of Bayes's theorem is undisputed, and Swinburne applies it with characteristic rigor. He concludes that "on the evidence considered so far, theism is neither very probable nor very improbable."[43] The evidence up to this point is evenly balanced. It is the evidence from religious experience that moves the balance of probability in favor of the existence of God. By adding the evidence from religious experience, Swinburne claims to move from a number of weak C-inductive arguments to an overall good P-inductive argument. The evidence from religious experience is, as Swinburne acknowledges, "crucial" to his argument.[44]

For Swinburne, therefore, some people make the decision to follow the Christian way not on the basis of any religious experience of their own, but on the basis of religious experiences that others claim to have had. Indeed, one must conclude that this is the case for most people. Swinburne's description of religious experience as "certain private and occasional manifestations by God to some men"[45] implies that religious experience is an unusual episode, an isolated event in which a privileged individual appropriates knowledge of a special reality that is not disclosed to the average person.

Before turning to Swinburne's understanding of religious faith, we should look once more at his distinctive treatment of the traditional arguments for the existence of God. I especially draw here from an essay by Otto Muck.[46]

As mentioned above, Swinburne rejects the ontological argument and maintains that none of the classical a posteriori arguments are good deductive arguments since their premises are far from generally accepted. Swinburne is hardly alone in questioning the usefulness of the ontological argument on the basis that its premises are a priori. As Muck points out, Thomas Aquinas argued that we do not know the essence of God and therefore we cannot show that existence belongs to it,[47] while Kant argued that existence is not a property that characterizes a concept and therefore it cannot be derived from conceptual analysis.[48] The ontological argument, at least in its Cartesian version, is strictly deductive, that is, analytic—it draws a conclusion from certain premises on the grounds that to deny the conclusion would be to contradict the premises—while the premises, since they are a priori, cannot be empirically verified.

Swinburne's dismissal of the view that the a posteriori arguments constitute good deductive arguments, however, represents a striking departure from the classical position. Against Swinburne, Muck argues that an a posteriori argument, because it includes among its premises general truths concerning the world of human experience, should not thereby be thought of as merely analytic. Muck points out that the traditional arguments for the existence of God were intended neither as deductive a priori arguments nor as inductive a posteriori arguments. Rather, they were intended as something between the two:

> This type of argument claims to be a logically sound deduction from what is found in experience. However, such an argument has other assumptions, not necessarily expressed. It is clear that the argument derives its strength from an assumed general principle, e.g. *omne autem quod movetur, ab alio movetur.*[49] Such principles were not analytic according to Thomas's thinking but expressed general truths concerning the world of human experience. So it was never claimed that one could conclude to the existence of God from experience alone; the general principle was also required for the cogency of the argument.[50]

It is this type of assumed general principle—everything that is moved is moved by another—that is far from generally accepted, according to Swinburne, and on this account he rejects the usefulness of deductive a posteriori arguments.

Swinburne makes much of the similarities between his approach and that of Thomas Aquinas, yet his decision to remove from the argument the assumed general principles in Thomas's arguments represents a complete departure from the Scholastic position. For Thomas, without the general principle, that is, without the rule according to which the argument is to be conducted, there is no argument. From Scripture and the tradition of the church Thomas believes that God has created the world *ex nihilo*, out of nothing. The principle that anything that is moved is moved by something else, together with his belief in creation, leads him to conclude that there must be an ultimate mover, or "God." Thomas, of course, uses Scripture throughout the *Summa Theologiae* and never relies solely on philosophical arguments. Through the application of principles or rules, the arguments enable him to explore the relationship between God and the world, as revealed in Scripture, in terms that are philosophically coherent.

Swinburne's complaint is that the assumed principle cannot be known with certainty; it can only be known with some degree of probability, however high that degree of probability might be. Hence, arguments that include such principles among their premises are useful as inductive arguments rather than deductive ones. But what does Swinburne mean by "useful?" Is Swinburne using the classical arguments for the same purpose as they were used by the Scholastics? Swinburne's working premise is that Christian theology, like natural science, is concerned with phenomena and the meaning and justification of theories that explain these phenomena. The theory that explains all observable phenomena is the theory "that God probably exists"; God is essentially "explanation."

The classical a posteriori arguments for God's existence also deal in explanation of phenomena. As Muck comments, the classical arguments proceed "from a reflection on the things of experience as exhibiting both signs of contingency, and perfections, by means of a principle that what is contingent requires explanation, to a being which grounds the things of experience, but itself has no signs of contingency requiring further explanation and contains the perfections."⁵¹ A general principle underlies the classical arguments: That which is contingent requires an explanation. "Contingent" here means depending for its existence or for its self-explanation upon that which is other than itself. There are several parts to this argument. First, since the phenomena of experience provide evidence of contingency, then according to the principle that what is contingent requires explanation, they point to a being that grounds the contingent. Second, that which grounds cannot itself be contingent since if it were, it would itself require explanation and so could not be the ultimate explanation. Third, since the phenomena of experience provide evidence of perfections, then according to the principle that what is contingent requires explanation, they point for their explanation to a more excellent perfection, which they reflect and in which they participate.

The principle that the being which grounds the things of experience cannot itself be contingent means that what the Scholastics were concerned with was an ultimate explanation, in a unique sense of this phrase. The argument from contingency to explanation deals with an explanation that is "ultimate." The concern is to find ways of talking about the ultimate, or God, in ways that are philosophically sound, that is, in ways that do not make God part of the fabric of the universe as God would be if, for example, God were "moveable." Swinburne, on the other hand, is engaged in an attempt to include God in the realm of things that can be scientifically proven. In terms of the Scholastics' endeavor, Swinburne is not using rational thought to articulate the transcendence of God in ways that are philosophically sound; instead he is looking for scientific evidence for the existence of God. But such an attempt cannot uphold the notion of God's transcendence, as conceived by the Scholastics, since it does treat of God as though God were part of the fabric of the universe.

The Rationalist Defense of Faith

So far the focus has been on Swinburne's account of God and its failure to uphold the classical notion of God's transcendence. Nonetheless, references to his account of humans have also provided a limited insight into his anthropology. As a rationalist, Swinburne unsurprisingly depicts the human subject as at the controlling center of the act of knowing, that is, able to understand things by means of its own intellect. Less obviously, he implies that human freedom is dependent on a degree of human nescience. Finally, he does not hold that religious experience belongs to general human experience, nor does he hold that the experience of God is mediated by the senses. Swinburne's understanding of faith must be examined in the light of this anthropology.

In *Faith and Reason,* the third book of his trilogy, Swinburne moves from a defense of theism in general to a defense of Christian faith in particular. In defense of Christianity, Swinburne's scientific method remains consistent. He does not seek to put forward a conclusive argument in favor of Christian discipleship; he merely seeks to persuade us that what is specifically proposed for belief by the Christian Church is more probably true than "the alternative." In the matter of adherence to Christianity rather than to another religion, just as in the matter of holding a theistic belief in the first place, he regards the fact that one is dealing with probability rather than certainty not as a matter of regret but as a positive advantage. The reason lies in his view of the relationship between belief and faith. Swinburne's aim to promote true belief is grounded in a more fundamental aim to promote faith. While "it matters greatly that one should have a true belief about whether there is a God, what He is like and what He has done . . . the virtue which the Christian religion commends is not propositional belief but . . . 'faith'."[52] Faith, in Swinburne's view, involves an element of trust that precludes certainty.

Faith is defined as "faith in a person or persons, God (or Christ) characterized as possessing certain properties and having done certain actions; and secondarily in some of the deeds which He has done, and the good things which He has provided and promised."[53] The preposition "in" is important here, signifying trust. To have faith *in* a person is to put one's trust in a person; to have faith *in* what has been promised is to put one's trust in that promise. Faith incorporates activity. Swinburne interprets the activity, or the living out, of faith as dependent upon true belief. "There are . . . two important concepts which come into definitions of faith . . . these are the concept of believing that so-and-so, e.g. that there is a God; and the concept of acting on the assumption that (or acting as if) so-and-so, e.g. that there is a God."[54] Thus faith, for Swinburne involves propositional belief and trust: "believing that" and "acting on the assumption that." Consequently, his defense of Christian faith has two parts. First, he attempts to defend the rationality of belief in the truth-claims of the Christian church; second, he attempts to defend the rationality of acting on the assumption that these claims *are* true.

The first part of Swinburne's strategy is likewise twofold. In examining the propositions that are set out for belief by the Christian Church, he attempts to defend the rationality of believing that these claims are true. At the same time, he seeks to determine the minimum level at which this particular type of belief needs to operate for the believer to engage in the second aspect of faith—to act on the assumption that these claims are true. He argues that according to the evidence we possess, these truth claims are probably true, and if they are probably true then it is rational to believe in them. "[T]o believe a proposition," he states, "is to believe it more probable than any alternative."[55] There are two ways of understanding "alternative" here.

> The normal alternative to a proposition is its negation. To believe that p is to believe that p is more probable than not-p. But the alternatives to a proposition may be narrower than the negation. In that case to believe that p is to believe that p is more probable than each of these alternatives q, r, s, etc. but not necessarily more probable than their disjunction. It follows from this that there are different things which believing a creed such as the Nicene Creed might amount to. First, it might be a matter of believing each item of the Creed to be more probable than its negation. Thus, understanding "I believe *in* one God, Father Almighty, maker of Heaven and Earth and of all things visible and invisible" as "I believe that there is one God who is Father Almighty, Maker of Heaven and Earth and of all things visible and invisible", we may in turn, understand this as "I believe that it is more probable that there is a God who is Father Almighty, Maker of Heaven and Earth, and of all things visible and invisible, than that there is not". And so on for each item of the Creed....
>
> Secondly, believing a creed such as the Nicene Creed might be a matter of believing each item of the Creed to be more probable

than each of a number of specific heretical or non-Christian alternatives. Someone affirming his belief in "the resurrection of the body" may be claiming that it is more probable that humans rise embodied than that (as some other religions claimed) they have an everlasting new life in a disembodied state.[56]

Swinburne does not consider that "a strong belief" is necessary to pursue the Christian way of life. In fact, he maintains, it would be unreasonable of the Christian Church to "insist that, to be a Christian, someone must believe that the Creed as a whole is more probable than its negation."[57] A sufficient requirement for membership of a Christian church, in Swinburne's view, is to believe that the propositions of the creed as a whole are more probable than the alternatives with which the propositions are contrasted, including the creeds of other religions.[58] Thus Swinburne seems to say that for a person to become a Christian, the minimum requirement is to believe that the probability of Jesus being the Lord is greater than the probability of Mohammed being the Prophet. Such a view is difficult to reconcile with the more traditional one: that the Christian way, at its most basic, is a response to Jesus, who calls one to follow him, and that it is God's Word, spoken in Jesus Christ, that calls forth the response "I believe." What sets Swinburne's approach apart from the traditional view is the notion that it is possible for a person with no religious experience to follow the Christian way. And for Swinburne, such a person is not an exception.

It comes as no surprise that Swinburne regards the items of a creed as open to the same type of scrutiny as the premises of a scientific hypothesis. However, what is most revealing in this attitude toward the Nicene Creed is the cost paid in terms of religious experience when the human being is understood first and foremost as an independent and rational being. Religious experience has become an unusual episode, an isolated event in which a privileged individual appropriates knowledge of a special reality. For the generality of human beings there is no sense of contact with a mystery that pervades the whole of creation, yet cannot be grasped. Nor is there any question of the experience of God being mediated by the liturgical recitation of the creed. Absent, too, is the notion that one affirms one's faith out of love, or out of wonder. Although Swinburne acknowledges that, according to Christian doctrine, "God is anxious to have friendship with man,"[59] no allowance is made in his philosophical discussion for the teaching that it is God, in Jesus Christ, who takes the initiative to draw the human being to God's self. With Swinburne, it is always the human being who takes the initiative in relation to God: the human being calculates that God probably exists, calculates that the Christian way is more likely to be true than the alternatives, and makes the decision to follow the Christian way in order to obtain salvation.

The second part of Swinburne's strategy is to defend the rationality of acting on the assumption that the propositions of Christian faith are true. If such propositions can be proved to be probably true, then granted it is rational to act upon that assumption. With regard to both propositional belief and trust, for Swinburne, judgments of probability are determinative. However, different levels of probability are appropriate in justifying the different aspects of faith, namely, believing in truth claims and acting as if these claims were true. Having a "belief that" a proposition is true is a matter of judging that whatever is proposed for belief is more probable than not, or is more probable than some proposed alternative. Yet one may believe that something is not very probable and still "act on the assumption that" it is true, because of the desirability of the rewards to be gained if it is true and because there is some probability that it is true. The motive for faith, it would seem, is self-interest. According to Swinburne, "belief that" is involuntary, in the sense that it depends on the view one takes of the evidence for the truth claim. However, "acting on the assumption that" is voluntary in that it involves decisions regarding the way in which one will inquire into religious truth and so acquire new evidence, and in that it involves acting voluntarily on one's beliefs or assumptions. "[A]cting on the assumption that He [God] will provide for us what we want or need" is what Swinburne understands by trusting in God.[60]

For the Christian, to trust in God is to live a supremely worthwhile life, guided by the Christian creed. The Christian way is one of generous action, generous to God and generous to other human beings. It involves friendship with God, giving God the worship and obedience that God deserves, and, after due penitence, being forgiven by and reconciled with God. It involves serving other human beings in both their bodily and spiritual needs. When Swinburne addresses the question of why a person should follow the Christian way of generous action, as always, judgments of probability are determinative. "Believing that" is involuntary in the sense that it depends directly on the evidence. But what persuades a person to acquire evidence in the first place and then to act upon the belief that results? Swinburne's reply is that it is in a person's interests to do so, in order to obtain salvation for oneself. Once again, his argument is explicable only when the calculation of one's best interests is paramount and takes place in the complete absence of any religious experience.

Swinburne gives three reasons for pursuing a religious way of life: "to render proper worship and obedience to any God or gods there may be, to attain one's own salvation and to help others to attain theirs."[61] Swinburne is sensitive to the criticism that his view of purpose of faith might be construed as selfish and thus un-Christian. "It is sometimes suggested that pursuing a religious way in order to secure one's own salvation is selfish. A religion of generous love such as Christianity would surely not encourage its pursuit for this motive? According, for example, to D. Z. Phillips, a person who pursued a religious way in order to gain salvation for himself would have missed the point of religion." Swinburne's reply is that it must be good to seek to make oneself saintly and to preserve oneself as such to eternity, and that according to Christian and most other views, to seek one's own salvation can never be at the cost of another's well being. "If it is good that I should improve my capacities . . . —as surely it is; and if it is good that I should seek to prolong them . . . —as surely it is; *a fortiori* it must be good that I should seek to make myself a saintly and generous person and to preserve such a being for eternity."[62]

What strikes the reader most forcibly about these assertions, apart from their Pelagian tone, is their unusually self-centered nature. Swinburne's argument is focused on gaining advantage for oneself, without any balancing reference to the way in which self-interest might be compatible with the Christian insistence on self-denial. While Swinburne does talk about performing generous actions for the sake of others, there is no discussion of the concepts of losing one's life in order to find it, of giving oneself over in love, of dying to the self, and so on. As a result, the picture painted of the human being is that of an isolated individual so totally taken up with reasoned action that there is no room for the giving over of the self that is necessary not merely for Christian discipleship but also, one may argue, for healthy human relationships.

In this context it is interesting to note Swinburne's appeal to the decree on justification of the Council of Trent, *De justificatione*, in support of his claim that it is not wrong for a person to seek to gain eternal salvation.[63] *De justificatione* indeed states that it is not wrong for persons to seek to gain their eternal salvation by their good works. Human beings are justified by the saving work of Jesus Christ, who graciously calls them to respond by their good works, and on their works they will be judged. Not only was the Catholic Church setting out here its teachings on justification, but the decree served to distance its teachings from the Reformers who taught that justification was by faith alone. But *De justificatione* can hardly be said to support Swinburne's position. Chapter 6 explicitly states that "whoever would draw near to God must believe that he exists and that he rewards those who seek him." The notion that one could seek one's own salvation on the basis of a calculation that God probably exists would be anathema to the theologians of the Counter-Reformation, as well as those of the Reformation.

The Results of a Rationalist Approach

Swinburne, as already indicated, supports his method and in some cases his arguments with references to the authorities of the late medieval period. It is important to stress, however, that up to and including the Council of Trent there was no question of proving the existence of God so that people could practice Christianity on the basis of evidence. The medieval theologians held that there were teachings that could be proved and teachings that could not, and that being a Christian meant believing those that could not be proved as well as those that could. God could "be known with certainty from the things that were created through the natural light of human reason," but it pleased God to be known "in another and a supernatural way," because God has ordained the human being to a "supernatural end, viz., to share in the good things of God which utterly exceed the intelligence of the human mind."[64] Theologians such as Thomas classified truths of faith according to whether they could be discovered by natural reason or whether they could be known only through the revelation of God, but there was no question of providing evidence for the existence of God (a truth that could be discovered by reason) as a prerequisite for faith in Jesus Christ, the only-begotten Son of God. And Thomas could never allow, as does Swinburne, that the existence of God could be discussed usefully outside the context of God's self-revelation in Jesus Christ. In the light of Thomas's categories, an insistence on providing evidence for all of those things that are proposed for belief should be treated with great caution. Even the early Christian apologists did not regard a defense of Christian faith as a proof of the validity of its claims. They merely argued that to believe in these claims, which could not themselves be proved, was a rational thing to do.

Swinburne's way of understanding the need to provide evidence in matters of faith has no precedent in premodern Christian thought. The sort of "proof" that Swinburne has sought for God's existence has been "scientific." God's existence is posited as the explanation for things that can be observed in creation, but as such, God is no longer understood as the ultimate explanation of all that is. Swinburne's "scientific" understanding of an ultimate explanation is unable to cope adequately with the notion of God's transcendence. Indeed, in treating knowledge of God as similar to knowledge of a finite object, Swinburne exhibits a certain blindness to the philosophical problem of how the finite human being can be said to apprehend the infinite God.

With respect to the anthropology underlying Swinburne's approach, the average human person is not represented as enjoying the experience of God or as capable of religious experience. The impression that in Swinburne's philosophy the human being is not essentially a spiritual being is strengthened by the focus on the necessity of calculating probabilities in order to know how to act in such a way as to secure one's maximum advantage.

Swinburne's religious epistemology is also problematic insofar as the experience of God, which may occur, is described as an experience unmediated by the senses. However, this calls into question not merely Swinburne's *religious* epistemology; on Swinburne's description, the senses may be bypassed in other experiences as well as in the experience of God. Furthermore, with the human subject at the center of the act of knowing and God at the outer reaches of the things that are known, it is evident that God is no longer understood as that which grounds or justifies the finite. Swinburne has nothing to say about how finite human knowledge is grounded.

Human beings, in Swinburne's system, lack a sense of God as the unfathomable mystery who calls each of them by name. And once the human self has taken up its position at the center of existence, once the human being no longer hears God's call, human freedom can no longer be identified with the freedom to surrender to the other, but is reduced first to the choice about whether to believe or not to believe something, and then to the choice about whether or not to act accordingly. Freedom is bound up with the freedom to assent to a probability.

Indeed, perhaps the most striking aspect of Swinburne's philosophy of religion is the role it accords the thinking subject. Epistemologically (as in every other respect), the human being is portrayed as the center of existence, and this portrayal affords Swinburne his rationalist credentials. The single assumption that underlies "rationalism," bringing with it its own set of problems, is that the human mind has within itself the resources to make sense of the finite world, including whatever facts or experiences are presented to it regarding what lies beyond the finite. For the rationalist, the human mind possesses an absolute autonomy.

In contrast to rationalism, the Christian faith teaches only a limited autonomy, since from its perspective the mind always derives its very existence from an external source. In Christian terminology, the mind always operates in the context of God's sustaining activity. Rationalism is demonstrably incompatible with Christianity because it effectively suggests that the human being, in making sense of itself, is not always sustained and informed by the activity of God. When the human mind is portrayed without qualification as independent of God, while at the same time the claim is made that the human mind can know God, the implication is that God is, as it were, brought into the orbit of human intellectual activity. It is as though God belongs within the scope of human intelligence.

At issue here is the paradox in the Christian claim that God, through Jesus Christ, may be known as an "object" of human thought, though by definition God—that which grounds human existence—cannot itself be known. The paradox is safeguarded only insofar as there is a full recognition that it is the unknown ground that discloses *itself*. Any suggestion that the unknown ground can be *discovered*, and that the human mind on its own initiative can perceive God, contradicts the very ultimateness that the word "God" is intended to convey. Does Swinburne, as it were, *bring* God into the orbit of human intellectual activity, or is he able to maintain the notion of God's absolute otherness even in discussion of God's self-disclosure? He does the former. And on the answer to this question hang all the concerns of this present work: the transcendence of God and the nature of the God-world relationship, how human freedom—indeed how human being—may be understood, what it means to know God, and even what it means to know anything at all.

The introduction to this book laid out two problems for religious epistemology, the challenge to provide evidence and the challenge implied in the mediation of our knowledge by finite reality. Swinburne understands the threat to religious belief purely in terms of the need for evidence. In response to this threat, he reasserts the role of the metaphysical in religious epistemology with what he considers to be rational, scientific arguments. He concludes that it is possible to prove on the balance of probability that God exists. But, in a way typical of a rationalist defense of Christian faith, his position fails to acknowledge the problem of how the finite human being can be said to apprehend the infinite God. Thus, while Swinburne's defense is intended to provide evidence for the probable reality of God, it fails to articulate clearly God's transcendence. Typical as well is the failure of his philosophy to take into account the relational element in human experience, in other words, to accommodate the terms of the second challenge regarding the mediation of knowledge. Swinburne's defense has nothing to say regarding the way in which human knowledge is grounded or how it is mediated.

CHAPTER 2
Postliberalism and Lindbeck

Of the two, intimately connected epistemological challenges to Christian faith that are the topic of this study, the first stems from the view that it should be possible, through reasoned argument based on evidence of some sort, to justify belief in any truth that is professed. As indicated in chapter 1, Christian truths were traditionally grounded or justified in one of two ways. Certain truths, such as the doctrine of the Trinity, were accepted on authority, as having been revealed by God, while other truths, such as the existence of God, were grounded in the observable phenomena of the created world. From early on, the Church found rational thought entirely compatible with revelation. Justin Martyr, for example, saw Christian revelation as the divine fulfillment of philosophical thought.[1] Similarly, the Scholastics did not suppose that rational thought was overridden by accepting the truths of revelation—indeed, rational thought processes were necessary for their communication. The premodern tradition as a whole believed that revelation filled out what could be known from human experience. It was only with the Enlightenment that evidence was required for revelation itself.

The rationalist apologetic strategy adopted to meet this first challenge, as exemplified in the philosophy of Richard Swinburne, has tended to be deficient in two respects. It has exhibited a certain blindness to the general problem of how the finite human being can be said to apprehend the infinite God. If God, as other, as uncreated, or as ultimate reality, is beyond the limits of human comprehension, how can Christians claim experience or knowledge of God? Moreover, the quest for evidence runs the danger of denying God's transcendence, or complete otherness.

The second epistemological challenge is to reconcile the tension between the claims about the transcendent that are part of Christianity, and the recognition that human knowledge is conditioned by created realities. "Postliberal" responses to this challenge have been made by, among others, the theologians George Lindbeck and Ronald Thiemann.[2] Frequently grouped with them in the postliberal category are Hans Frei and Stanley Hauerwas. Common to all of these thinkers is the attempt to reinterpret Christian faith to take into account the conditioning of human knowing. Particularly influential in this regard are Lindbeck's *The Nature of Doctrine*[3] and Thiemann's *Revelation and Theology*.[4]

In many ways the theological positions of Lindbeck and Thiemann coincide, yet they differ significantly with regard to the justification of faith. For Lindbeck—as we shall see in this chapter—justification of faith is inappropriate. Although his argument allows the possibility of justification, it does so only because he wants his cultural-linguistic approach to religious belief to accommodate any kind of religious system, even a realist interpretation of religious propositions. Thiemann, similarly, has strong reservations regarding the justification of faith, but he holds that unless the doctrine of revelation can be justified, the whole basis of faith is lost. (Thiemann must therefore cope with a tension between his recognition that justification is needed and his Lutheran/Barthian heritage, with its history of suspicion regarding the justification of faith.)

Both Lindbeck and Thiemann reject "foundationalism," which, generally speaking, refers to the view that there are certain non-inferential, self-evident beliefs that serve as the foundation of all knowledge. Such beliefs are not established through the mediation of the finite world; they are simply "given." According to foundationalism, these foundational beliefs play a crucial role in the ability of the human mind to know God. The rejection of foundationalism in its many forms characterizes postliberalism in general. Thiemann's specific definition of foundationalism will be of interest in chapter 3. What is significant for the moment is that, for Lindbeck and Thiemann, all religious epistemology is foundationalist and therefore flawed.

While Thiemann on the whole confines his specific criticisms of foundationalist approaches to Protestant theology, those of George Lindbeck, whose declared motive is to facilitate ecumenism, are more far-reaching. By means of a fairly complex categorization, he attempts to sum up the broad range of Western religious epistemologies and challenge them all.[5] In the case of both Thiemann and Lindbeck, moreover, their criticism is not merely confined to this or that approach to religious epistemology but is intended as a comprehensive critique of them all. Thiemann and Lindbeck, as well as other postliberal theologians such as Frei and Hauerwas, intend to move the discussion of our knowledge of God to new ground.

In turning now in detail to the arguments of George Lindbeck and, in chapter 3, to those of Ronald Thiemann, my intention is to outline the strengths and weaknesses of representative postliberal positions on epistemological challenges to religious belief. I do not attempt to survey postliberal theologies in general, although the results in these two case studies can readily be extended to other postliberal theologies.

Lindbeck's classification of contemporary arguments in religious epistemology is complex, but broadly speaking it can be summed up in terms of two positions, both of which he opposes. The first is a conservative propositional or doctrinal model of revelation—a "rationalist" or "cognitivist" model; the second is what he calls the "liberal" or "experiential-expressivist" approach to revelation, which treats doctrines as symbols with cognitive import.[6] His approach to these two main kinds of arguments—the rationalist and the liberal—will be considered in turn.

Lindbeck's Critique of the Rationalist Approach

Lindbeck's criticism of the rationalist position is that it assumes that doctrines of the Christian Church are intended primarily to convey knowledge about God. The most significant claim of his theology is that Christian doctrines are not intended primarily to teach what has been revealed in Christ about God (nor are they primarily to be regarded as expressive symbols), but rather they are intended to have what Lindbeck calls a regulative function. (Ronald Thiemann, discussed in the next chapter, also acknowledges the regulative function of doctrine, but it is by no means his primary focus.)

Lindbeck advocates an approach to religious doctrines according to which "emphasis is placed on those respects in which religions resemble languages together with their correlative forms of life and are thus similar to cultures (insofar as these are understood semiotically as reality and value systems—that is, as idioms for the construing of reality and the living of life). The function of church doctrines that becomes most prominent in this perspective is their use, not as expressive symbols or as truth claims, but as communally authoritative rules of discourse, attitude, and action."[7] Lindbeck thus treats religion essentially as "language," bearing in mind the mutual relationship between a language and the way of life that corresponds to and is shaped by the language. A religious language is similar to a culture in that, like a culture, it provides the framework within which reality may be interpreted and it shapes the way in which those who use the language live their lives. Thus, "a religion can be viewed as a kind of cultural and/or linguistic framework or medium that shapes the entirety of life and thought."[8] Doctrines then function primarily as rules, which are authoritative for everybody who works by that particular religious language, and which determine the shape of their discourse, their basic attitudes, and the way in which they live their lives.

Although Lindbeck does not discuss Swinburne explicitly, his "rule theory" directly applies to Swinburne's position. In response to Swinburne's arguments that what is specifically proposed for belief by the Christian Church is more probably true than the alternative,[9] Lindbeck would reply that Swinburne has misunderstood the primary role of Christian doctrine. Swinburne argues that the belief about God conveyed by a collection of propositions taken together (the Christian creed) is most probably true, so that by believing these propositions one most probably has true knowledge about God. One may then choose to act according to one's belief. Lindbeck allows that such doctrines may convey knowledge about God, but they may also function perfectly well without conveying knowledge about God. Hence someone like Swinburne has misunderstood what they are really for. Furthermore, according to Lindbeck, any success that Swinburne or anyone else has in persuading people that what is proposed for religious belief is probably true will depend entirely on the particular circumstances of those whom they seek to persuade.

Swinburne's theology fits neatly into the first of the two types of contemporary theological theories recognized and criticized by Lindbeck. Swinburne belongs to the "rationalist" or "cognitivist" category as opposed to the "liberal" or "experiential-expressivist" category. (Lindbeck also recognizes a third category, which combines aspects of both the cognitivist theory and of the experiential-expressivist theory.) The cognitivist theory "emphasizes the cognitive aspects of religion and stresses the ways in which church doctrines function as informative propositions or truth claims about objective realities. Religions are thus thought of as similar to philosophy or science as these were classically conceived. This was the approach of traditional orthodoxies (as well as of many heterodoxies), but it also has certain affinities to the outlook on religion adopted by much modern Anglo-American analytic philosophy with its preoccupation with the cognitive or informational meaningfulness of religious utterances."[10] Here, Lindbeck might very well be writing with Swinburne in mind. Swinburne, as we have seen, uses scientific methods; he examines different creeds to assess whether on balance it is probable that they reveal the objective reality of God; and his work is profoundly shaped by the particular brand of analytic philosophy that flourished at Oxford. Against the cognitivists—those who think like Swinburne—Lindbeck maintains that doctrines are not primarily intended to function as informative propositions or truth claims about objective realities.

Yet Lindbeck does not deny altogether that the truth claims or doctrines of religious faith can supply objective knowledge about God; rather, he insists that it is not their primary function to do so. In allowing the possibility of objective knowledge, however, Lindbeck does not thereby suggest that Christianity appeals to reason in the claims that it makes about the transcendent. The objective knowledge in question derives not from reason but from a way of life that corresponds to the ultimately real. Lindbeck maintains that "propositional truth and falsity characterize ordinary religious language when it is used to mold lives through prayer, praise, preaching, and exhortation. It is only on this level that human beings linguistically exhibit their truth or falsity, their correspondence or lack of correspondence to the Ultimate Mystery."[11]

Lindbeck's highly nuanced understanding of truth repays close scrutiny. He presents three ways of understanding truth, the first two of which he rejects and the third of which he affirms. First, for more traditional orthodox Christians—Swinburne would fall into this category—propositional truth is a matter of correspondence, which Lindbeck also refers to as "ontological truth." Quoting from Bernard Lonergan, Lindbeck says of this group, "Those who are to some degree traditionally orthodox understand the propositional truth that they attribute to religious statements as a function of the ontological correspondence or 'isomorphism' of the 'structure of the knowing and the structure of the known.'"[12] Second, for those in the "experiential-expressivist" group, truth is "a function of symbolic efficacy" and truth is equated with efficacy.[13] Third, for those adopting a cultural-linguistic outlook, truth is conceived in terms of the adequacy of the categories of different religions. "Adequate categories are those which can be made to apply to what is taken to be real, and which therefore make possible, though they do not guarantee, propositional, practical, and symbolic truth." This truth of "categorical adequacy"[14] Lindbeck also refers to as "intrasystematic truth" or "the truth of coherence."[15]

In order "to do justice to the actual speech and practice of religious people,"[16] Lindbeck must show that the cultural-linguistic outlook can accommodate the notion that propositional truth is a matter of correspondence. Lindbeck allows that "conformity of the self to God can . . . be pictured in epistemologically realistic fashion as involving a correspondence of the mind to divine reality,"[17] although to Lindbeck this notion of conformity is secondary to the notion of moral conformity. Lindbeck's approach is descriptive: he observes that certain religious systems do claim that the propositions of faith have a cognitive as well as a regulative role.

Lindbeck argues that the cultural-linguistic outlook is not, in itself, incompatible with some version of correspondence. He also holds that for a religious statement to be true, there must be an element of practical conformity to the truth that is claimed. Thus, "the crusader's battle cry 'Christus est Dominus' . . . is false when used to authorize cleaving the skull of the infidel."[18] However, in spite of the "modest cognitivism or propositionalism"[19] of the cultural-linguistic approach, his main stress is on the "performative" or ethical dimension of religious utterances.

Lindbeck states that a religion *as it is actually lived* may be pictured as a single proposition. "It is a true proposition to the extent that its objectivities are interiorized and exercised by groups and individuals in such a way as to conform them in some measure in the various dimensions of their existence to the intimate reality and goodness that lies at the heart of things. It is a false proposition to the extent that this does not happen."[20]

Lindbeck describes this conformity of the self to God through the religious statement as "performatory," borrowing the term from J. L. Austin. Lindbeck, however, moves beyond Austin's self-consciously plain definition of "performative" to a nuanced interpretation that would doubtless dismay Austin.[21] Austin himself alludes to a performative utterance as follows: "I want to discuss a kind of utterance which looks like a statement and grammatically . . . could be classed as a statement, which is not nonsensical, and yet is not true or false. . . . Furthermore, if a person makes an utterance of this sort we should say that he is *doing* something rather than merely *saying* something."

The crucial point for Austin is that in saying what one does, one actually performs that action. For example, when one says the words "I will" in an appropriate context one performs the act of marrying.[22] Lindbeck suggests that a religious utterance might likewise be construed as "performative." Further, when the religious utterance is regarded as "performative," it might then be possible to talk of a correspondence to reality that is created by the religious utterance itself. Thus, "a religious utterance, one might say, acquires the propositional truth of ontological correspondence . . . insofar as it is a performance, an act or deed, which helps create that correspondence."

Lindbeck admits that this does not occur "in non-religious performative speech, where . . . utterances cannot simultaneously function both performatively and propositionally." Yet he takes up Austin's example of an utterance in marriage and gives it a new interpretation, one that has both propositional and performative elements: he suggests that "in a marriage genuinely made in heaven, the earthly promises would produce a 'propositional' correspondence of one reality to another."[23] Thus, according to Lindbeck's novel interpretation, it could be said that the truth of a religious utterance lies in "a way of being in the world" or performance, and it is the performance that *creates* whatever correspondence may be deemed to exist.

Lindbeck's interpretation of Thomas Aquinas in this context is telling, in two respects. In the first place, Lindbeck argues that in the religious utterance, the Scholastic notion of truth as "an adequation of the mind to the thing (*adaequatio mentis ad rem*) . . . can be pictured as part and parcel of a wider conformity of the self to God":[24]

> [The] performatory conformity of the self to God can . . . be pictured in an epistemologically realistic fashion as involving a correspondence of the mind to divine reality. This is true, at any rate, when one conceives of this correspondence in as limited a fashion as does, for example, Thomas Aquinas. There seems to be no reason, in other words, why cultural-linguistic theories of religion need exclude, even though they do not imply, the modest cognitivism or propositionalism represented by at least some classical theists. . . .[25]

In the second place, Lindbeck argues, Thomas's concept of analogical language about God affords no real insight into the nature of God:

> Aquinas holds that although in statements about God the human mode of signifying (*modus significandi*) does not correspond to anything in the divine being, the signified (*significatum*) does. Thus, for example, when we say that God is good, we do not affirm that any of our concepts of goodness (*modi significandi*) apply to him, but rather that there is a concept of goodness unavailable to us, viz., God's understanding of his own goodness, which does apply. What we assert, in other words, is that "God is good" is meaningful and true, but without knowing the meaning of "God is good" . . .
>
> What, however, is the function of truth claims about God if their cognitive content is as minimal as has just been suggested? If we do not know how God is good (viz., the *modus significandi*), then we cannot derive any nontautologous consequences from the affirmation that he is good.[26]

Undoubtedly a strength of Lindbeck's ambitious project is his insistence that religious beliefs are conditioned by created realities. And he is right to say that for a religious statement to be true, there must be an element of practical conformity to the truth that is claimed. But close inspection indicates that his position does not allow even the modest cognitivism that he claims for it. In his interpretation of Thomas, for example, Lindbeck seems to have so reduced what he understands by a "modest cognitivism" that it counts for nothing. In explaining how Thomas deals with the attribution to God of perfections such as "good," Lindbeck concludes that it is not possible to derive any nontautologous consequences from the affirmation that God is good. He thus implies that in Thomas's view there can be no real insight into the nature of God. Yet Lindbeck fails to do justice to the positive element of Thomas's teaching on analogy.

In *Summa Theologiae* 1a, 13, 3, Thomas says that there are two things to be considered: the way of signifying (*modum significandi*) and the perfections themselves that are signified (*perfectiones ipsas significatas*). Insofar as the way of signifying is concerned, "the words are used inappropriately." Insofar as the perfections signified are concerned, they "are used literally of God, and in fact more appropriately than they are used of creatures, for these perfections belong primarily to God and only secondarily to others." Lindbeck's interpretation implies that the first statement contradicts the second: if the first is true, the second cannot be true. In Thomas's view, however, the goodness (for example) in the human being has been received from the source of goodness—God. Goodness describes God more appropriately than it describes creatures. In knowing what goodness means for a creature, the human being has a real insight into what goodness means for God, since God is the source from which human goodness flows. God is known from the perfections that flow from him and are to be found in creatures. Although these perfections are to be found in a transcendent way in God, they nonetheless afford real insight into God's nature.

Like Swinburne, Lindbeck fails to understand how, according to Thomas, we may talk meaningfully about God. Swinburne does not recognize that the insight into God's nature afforded by analogical language is something quite different from the insight that one might gain into the nature of a created existent. Lindbeck, by contrast, is conscious that this difference must be respected and therefore denies that the attribution of perfections affords any real insight into the nature of God.

In effect, Lindbeck's position implies that propositions of faith cannot convey knowledge that has been revealed in Christ about God. As a result, none of his attempts to accommodate the view that they do convey knowledge about God are successful. Much of the time these attempts lead to ambiguity. For example, Lindbeck states that "it is only on this level [when propositions of faith are used to mold lives through prayer, praise, preaching, and exhortation] that human beings linguistically exhibit their truth or falsity, their correspondence or lack of correspondence to the Ultimate Mystery.[27] Lindbeck can interpret this to mean that when Christians use the language of prayer, the correspondence to reality consists in the fact that they are praying, while allowing others to think that the correspondence lies in the prayer that is said.

Given the absence of a consistent unequivocal assertion that the propositions of faith afford knowledge revealed in Christ about God, Lindbeck's approach is unable to avoid the charge of relativism. With reference to performative utterances, for example, Lindbeck claims that it might be possible to talk of a correspondence to reality that is created by the religious utterance itself: a religious utterance might acquire the truth of ontological correspondence insofar as it is a performance that helps to create the correspondence. If it is the performance (uttering the proposition) that creates the ontological correspondence (the truth of the proposition), then it must be the case that a different performance (that is to say, uttering a different proposition) would create a different ontological correspondence (that is to say, a different truth). The implication is that truth is relative to the proposition that is uttered.

Lindbeck's Critique of the Liberal "Experiential" Tradition

Lindbeck offers a scathing critique of what he terms the "liberal" or "experiential-expressivist" approach to revelation, which is based on the notion that there is a religious experience common to all human beings. Kant, for Lindbeck, is a pivotal figure. When Kant demolished the metaphysical and epistemological foundations of "cognitivitism" or a "cognitive-propositional" view of Christian faith, he posed an overwhelmingly difficult challenge that sent Christian theology off in a false direction. The most significant result of this theological redirection, according to Lindbeck, is the experiential-expressivist tradition. Kant "did not replace the view of religion he had undermined with a more adequate one"; rather, his "reduction of God to a transcendental condition (albeit a necessary one) of morality" left religion intolerably impoverished. "The breach was filled, beginning with Schleiermacher," with what Lindbeck terms "experiential-expressivism."[28]

The experiential-expressivist tradition, according to Lindbeck, interprets the public features of religion as derived from internal experience. Religious doctrines, like the other public features of religion, are the result of reflection upon an initially prereflective experience in the depths of the self, where contact with whatever is finally important to religion takes place. Religions are "products of those deep experiences of the divine (or the self, or the world) which most of us are accustomed to thinking of as peculiarly religious."[29] The public features of religion, as well as expressing the objectification of the prereflective experience, also evoke that experience. In the experiential tradition, therefore, doctrines are expressive symbols, both expressing and evoking the primary experience. Of course Lindbeck, as discussed above, holds an altogether different view, according to which the function of doctrines, like that of all other public features of religion, is not to express and evoke "religious experiences" but to regulate human living.

Lindbeck argues that in the experiential tradition the thinking subject is treated as an "isolated" subject, since contact with whatever is finally important to religion takes place "in the prereflective . . . depths of the self." As a result, religion becomes a highly private and individual matter. Lindbeck rejects the possibility that the isolation is overcome in the unity or commonality of the religious experience itself, by denying that any such a unity can be proved to exist. Yet the assumption of a common, single kind of religious experience, according to Lindbeck, is crucially important to the experiential tradition.

Once one accepts the idea that there is a core religious experience common to all humanity and that doctrines and other public features of religion are products of this core experience, it logically follows that the various religions are merely different ways of symbolizing one and the same core experience of the ultimate. Religions should therefore "respect each other, learn from each other, and reciprocally enrich each other."[30]

There is religion in general, which for the experiential-expressive form of religion is an individual quest for personal meaning; and there are the different religions, which are seen as multiple suppliers of different forms of a single commodity needed for transcendent self-expression and self-realization. Individuals, according to this view, meet God first in the depths of their souls and then, perhaps, choose to make a decision to become part of a tradition or join a church.[31] Theologians whose work is shaped by the desire to meet the needs for meaning, order, and transcendence are often fully aware, according to Lindbeck, that religion is inseparable from particular traditions and communities. "Nevertheless, the exigencies of communicating their messages in a privatistic cultural and social milieu lead them to commend public and communal traditions as optional aids in individual self-realization rather than as bearers of normative realities to be interiorized."[32]

Lindbeck cites Bernard Lonergan in particular as a representative of experiential-expressivism. According to Lindbeck, at least four of the six theses by which Lonergan summarizes his theory of religion in his *Method in Theology*[33] are characteristic of experiential-expressivism in general: First, different religions are diverse expressions or objectifications of a common core experience. It is this experience which identifies them as religions. Second, the experience, while conscious, may be unknown on the level of self-conscious reflection. Third, it is present in all human beings. And fourth, in most religions, the experience is the source and norm of objectifications: it is by reference to the experience that their adequacy or lack of adequacy is to be judged. Lonergan assumes, as do most experiential-expressivist theologians, that the scholarly study of religious phenomena on the whole supports the crucial affirmation of the basic commonality of religious experience.[34]

This assumption, according to Lindbeck, is unwarranted. Because its proponents claim that this core experience is common to a wide diversity of religions, it is difficult or impossible to specify its distinctive features; yet unless its distinctive features are specified, the assertion of commonality becomes logically and empirically vacuous. Lonergan, for example, grants that religious experience "varies with every difference of culture, class or individual"[35] and that there is no clear-cut evidence that religious experience conforms to the model he has set forth in his *Method in*

Theology;[36] nevertheless, he takes for granted that this model, which assumes the common nature of religious experience, best accommodates the evidence.

Lindbeck notes that Lonergan cites, in particular, arguments of Friedrich Heiler in support of the view that the so-called higher religions come from one and the same root experience of transcendence. Heiler found similarities in Christianity, Judaism, Islam, Zoroastrianism, Hinduism, Buddhism, and Taoism, both in terms of what they say about the supreme reality and in terms of the view that the path to the supreme reality involves repentance, self-denial, and so on.[37] Lindbeck objects on two counts to such efforts to show that all religions are basically similar. First, he observes that an adherent of an Eastern religion embarked on the same quest for similarities in world religions would come up with a different list; they would make Christianity sound rather like Taoism or Buddhism, for example, rather than vice versa. Second, and more important for Lindbeck, religions should be treated as similar to languages. What counts in determining similarities between languages are grammatical patterns, the ways of referring, and the semantic and syntactic structures of the languages. Analogously, what counts in determining similarities between religions are not the words in common, such as "love" and "God," but the distinctive patterns of story, belief, ritual, and behavior that give the common terms such as "love" and "God" their specific and sometimes contradictory meanings.

Given this view of what counts in religious belief, Lindbeck rejects the idea that one can be religious in general, before belonging to a specific religious group. According to Lindbeck's cultural-linguistic outlook, one can "no more be religious in general than one can speak language in general."[38]

For Lindbeck, Schleiermacher and the theological tradition influenced by Schleiermacher treat knowledge of God as given through a common core experience that is unmediated by the finite world and thus unmediated by culture or language in their broadest sense. As Lindbeck observes, even Lonergan admits that the concept of this common core experience is problematic:

> Lonergan . . . has theological reasons . . . for affirming the underlying unity of religious experience, but when looked at nontheologically,

this is the most problematic element in his, as in other, experiential-expressive theories. *Lonergan himself acknowledges that it is logically odd.* He speaks of it as an experience of love, but also admits that *it alone among inner, nonsensory experiences seems to be prior to all conceptualization or cognition.*[39]

According to Lindbeck, the theologian Karl Rahner also shares Lonergan's view that there is a core religious experience, which "precedes the distinction between subject and object."[40] Whether Lindbeck is right in aiming his criticism at Schleiermacher and Rahner will be discussed in chapters 5 and 6, respectively.

Lindbeck's main claim, as we have seen, is that Christian doctrines are primarily intended not to teach what has been revealed in Christ about God, but to have a regulative function in our behavior. He thus directly opposes the position taken by Swinburne. Lindbeck accepts that it is possible to affirm that religious propositions have a cognitive element, but he interprets this possibility in a sense so limited as to render the affirmation worthless. The propositions of Christian faith are not intended to supply knowledge about God, and thus there can be no question of providing any sort of evidence to justify their truth. Knowledge of the transcendent, mediated by the propositions of faith, results from a way of living in relation to the propositions. No exercise in rational thought regarding those propositions can supply such knowledge. He dismisses as totally irrelevant the type of exercise undertaken by Swinburne.

Lindbeck argues, moreover, that there is a basic contradiction underlying both the rationalist position and the experiential-expressivist position concerning the supposed ability of the human mind to refer to the transcendent and come to a knowledge of God. Insofar as Christianity makes claims to knowledge of the transcendent, he is not prepared to offer any kind of justification in support of such claims. He has no answer to give to those who believe that the truths of faith must be supported by some kind of evidence. He rejects this endeavor as contradicting the Lutheran tradition regarding justification and as opening the way to foundationalism.

CHAPTER 3

The Anti-foundationalism of Thiemann

The first challenge to Christian faith with which this book is concerned arose from the Enlightenment and is, in that sense, a modern challenge. The second challenge, which forces the Christian apologist to recognize the mediation of *all* knowledge, is of more recent origin. It is part of the postmodern enterprise, which maintains a critical stance toward the thinking of the modern period. Postliberal theologians such as George Lindbeck and Ronald Thiemann, who take seriously the mediation of all knowing, offer powerful analyses of the problems that have arisen when theologians try to meet the Enlightenment demand for evidence. This chapter initially examines the analyses put forward by Ronald Thiemann, in order to come to grips more fully with the epistemological problems of the modern period as seen through the eyes of postmodern theology, as well as to to shed further light on postliberal approaches. This examination will also provide an introduction to Thiemann's own constructive endeavor.

In Defense of Revelation

Swinburne, as we have seen, interprets the challenges that are posed to Christian faith in modern times as challenges to defend the rationality of belief in the existence of God. Thiemann, on the other

49

hand, assumes that God exists but takes as his task a defense of what he terms God's prevenience, that is, "faith's knowledge of God is a gift bestowed through God's free grace." The stress is on the priority of God: "thought and speech about God are not simply the free creations of human imagination but are developed in obedient response to God's prior initiative."[1] Thus, while Swinburne is concerned with the *existence* of God, Thiemann is concerned with the existence of *God*—the utterly other, who alone takes the initiative in the divine/human relationship. Thiemann interprets the challenges that are posed to Christian faith in modern times as challenges to defend the doctrine of revelation. At this level, therefore, he engages with the first challenge: the need to supply some sort of evidence for what is proposed for belief.

Compared with Lindbeck, Thiemann engages more fully with various positions that he criticizes and therefore has more to say about their underlying epistemologies. While Lindbeck is concerned with the function of doctrines generally, rather than the veracity of any single doctrine or set of doctrines, Thiemann offers a defense of the doctrine of revelation—indeed, he believes such a defense is vital for the survival of Christian faith. Thus Thiemann, unlike Lindbeck, is explicitly working out his theology from within the context of faith. Lindbeck's work may provide a useful tool for critical analysis, but for the purposes of inter-theological dialogue, Thiemann, not Lindbeck, acts as a conversation-partner.

Thiemann—a Lutheran and a Barthian—apparently sees no conflict between the distaste for apologetics characteristic of the tradition of Karl Barth, and his own view that the doctrine of revelation must be defended and backed up by some sort of evidence. For Thiemann, the very existence of Christianity, dependent as it is on God's self-revelation, is threatened by a concerted attack from within the Lutheran tradition on the notion of revelation. In his *Revelation and Theology*, Thiemann states that two "very early attacks on the notion of revelation come from European Lutherans who were reacting against the Calvinist categories which predominate in the modern theological discussion" and for illustration quotes from Werner Elert: "Nowhere [in the New Testament] is it said that God has revealed, reveals or will reveal himself."[2] Thiemann finds a "growing consensus among contemporary theologians," nicely captured by Stanley Hauerwas's remark that the "very idea that the Bible is revealed . . . is a claim that creates more trouble than it is worth."³ Gustaf Wingren, he notes, offers a sustained polemic against Barth's "unbiblical" employment of the notion of revelation. For Thiemann, in short, the doctrine of revelation is under serious attack, and a defense of this doctrine is a necessary defense of the Barthian tradition, which would suffer complete collapse without the notion of revelation.

Thiemann thus equates a defense of religious belief with a defense of the doctrine of revelation. But as a Lutheran and a Barthian, he cannot support his claims with evidence from natural theology. A rationalist defense is out of the question. Knowledge of God, according to Thiemann, comes about only through revelation:

> Despite important differences in rhetoric Luther and Barth give common witness to the central Christian conviction that faith's knowledge of God is a gift of God's grace. Whatever their manifest flaws, modern doctrines of revelation have attempted to restate that central Christian conviction. Luther's insistence that faith "is not a human work but utterly a divine gift" has been recast in the modern discussion to stress that faith's knowledge is not a natural human possession but a new possibility granted through the graciousness of the giver. Both positions stress the *prevenience* of God's grace, the conviction that we are enabled to have access to God solely through God's prior action.⁴

Although many Protestant theologians since the 1960s have argued against the notion of revelation, all who attempt to defend "God's prevenience," according to Thiemann, are in fact concerned either explicitly or implicitly with the doctrine of revelation. In particular, he has in mind those who seek to bypass the notion of revelation and defend "God's prevenience" by asserting the universality of a "religious dimension" of human experience. Such arguments, he claims, serve as "functional equivalents" to doctrines of revelation in that they are "theoretical justifications for Christian belief in the priority of God's gracious reality."⁵ "The problem of revelation is not simply a problem associated with particular outmoded objectivist metaphors for speaking of God's reality," Thiemann observes. "The problem is whether *any* coherent argument can be made which establishes God's prior reality."⁶ Since Thiemann regards "foundationalism"—by which he means any theory that knowledge of God is based on a foundational, intuitive contact with the transcendent—as the source of incoherence in all areas of modern Protestant religious epistemology, his aim is to show "how nonfoundational resources can be used to defend belief in God's prevenience."⁷ He does this by attempting to construct a coherent argument that is removed from what he understands as religious epistemology. He does not intend it to be an epistemological one.

Thiemann is clearly willing to provide evidence of some sort to defend the notion of God's prevenience. Yet his determination to use only "nonfoundational resources" as evidence alerts the reader to the fact that his overriding concern is not with the challenge to provide evidence. Thiemann must avoid the problems of foundationalism, with its underlying assumption that the finite human mind can apprehend the infinite God. And any evidence which he provides must allow for the fact that all human knowledge, including knowledge of God, is culturally and historically mediated. Thus his overriding concern is with the second epistemological challenge.

In illustrating the kind of positions he opposes, Thiemann points out that from the beginning of the eighteenth century through the 1960s, and markedly between the 1920s and 1960s, Protestant theologians have argued vigorously in order to justify Christian claims to revelation.⁸ On the one hand, they have assumed that claims to revelation must be "reasonable" in the sense of not being contrary to reason. On the other hand, they have argued that revelation designates a special category of truths accessible only through a unique mode of knowing. Since the knowledge of God that comes through faith comes about only through revelation, many of them have interpreted this to mean that the truths of revelation cannot result from the structuring processes of rational thought. Therefore knowledge of God must bypass the usual cognitive processes. Yet the theoretical justification for religious belief must be possible. It must be possible to show that to believe what has been revealed in Christ about God is not an irrational thing to do. It must be possible to use rational arguments to back up the claim that through faith there does come knowledge of God. To resolve this tension, they must demonstrate that while the truths of faith differ from truths that result from the processes of rational thought, they are nonetheless sufficiently similar to be amenable to the same type of rational justification.

According to Thiemann, however, the fragile balance between the distinctiveness of the truths of revelation and their similarity to truths known through ordinary uses of reason has proved almost impossible to maintain.[9] This is so whether the attempt has been made by those who seek to defend God's prevenience by asserting the universality of a "religious dimension" of human experience (in Lindbeck's terminology, the liberal or experiential-expressivist approach), or by those who accept the absolute contrast between revelation and autonomous reason while arguing that such an acceptance is not irrational (the so-called dialectical approach). Both approaches, Thiemann claims, are equally foundationalist.

Revelation as "Divine Impression"

Thiemann's criticism of Friedrich Schleiermacher's theology of revelation[10] is in many ways similar to Lindbeck's criticism of the liberal or experiential-expressivist tradition, which in fact was founded, as Lindbeck sees it, by Schleiermacher. Schleiermacher's theology is analyzed on its own terms in the next chapter. Here, however, our focus is on Thiemann's critique of Schleiermacher as a way of understanding Thiemann—putting aside the question of whether his account of Schleiermacher is complete or plausible.

Referring to Schleiermacher's *The Christian Faith*, Thiemann states that "Schleiermacher's belief in the basic compatibility of Christian faith and rational inquiry shows itself in his treatment of revelation."[11] The "key characteristic of revelation" for Schleiermacher "is that it originates from a divine source," and this is explained as an experience stemming from a divine origin, in contrast to ordinary experience:

> Schleiermacher . . . [appeals] to the peculiar quality of a divinely originating experience. Nonrevelatory experiences are apprehended by ordinary means of knowing. We synthesize new experiences through the normal categories which regulate our knowledge and action. The new becomes familiar through an inferential extension

of our previous ordinary experience. . . . Revelation, by contrast, occurs when we have an immediate experience of an other which we apprehend not inferentially but directly. Revelation can "only be apprehended . . . as a moment of the life of a thinking being who acts upon us directly as a distinctive existence by means of his total impression on us." Revelation is a self-conscious experience, but it does not directly engage our knowing and doing but our self-conscious states of feeling, i.e., our *immediate* self-consciousness.[12]

The immediate self-consciousness, beyond knowledge and action, is therefore precognitive. Revelation is "impressed" upon the human being in a way that bypasses the mediation of the created world. The immediacy of the feeling of absolute dependence establishes its extra-ordinary character, its divine origin:

Schleiermacher claims to have discerned the formal, universal, precognitive shape of piety-as-such, prior to its combination with particular historical or cultural elements. In historical experience the universal God-consciousness is always linked to some particular which gives each religious community its peculiar identity, but the essential shape of piety, the experience of absolute dependence, remains the same. That experience is one of feeling or immediate self-consciousness, and cannot be grasped under the ordinary categories which shape knowing and doing. The feeling of absolute dependence removes one from the world of particular times and places, of distinct subjects and objects, and allows an immediate relation to God through the transparent tissue of feeling.[13]

Thiemann maintains that for Schleiermacher, the plausibility of the Christian claim to revelation rests on the success of the argument which demonstrates the possibility of God-consciousness, the consciousness of being absolutely dependent, or, which is the same thing, of being in relation to God. But, Thiemann asks, can the self-evidence of this experience be established, in light of the fact that we are rarely infallible interpreters of our own feelings? Schleiermacher (still according to Thiemann) would doubtless argue that this immediate self-consciousness differs in kind from other experiences, but he fails to give a sufficiently clear account of the characteristics that mark an experience as self-evident. Thiemann also concludes that Schleiermacher does not adequately explain why an experience of absolute dependence should be taken to be an experience of God. Schleiermacher has moved, without proper justification, from a self-referential claim to a referential claim concerning a distinct other. The fact that, according to Schleiermacher, one *seems* to be encountering God can hardly suffice to justify a claim to revelation.

Thus, according to Thiemann, Schleiermacher's attempt to justify the Christian claim to revelation can succeed only if it is possible to make a distinction between inferential and non-inferential experiences and beliefs (for example, between immediate and non-immediate states of consciousness). Schleiermacher must also successfully defend the claim that non-inferential experiences are direct and immediate and thus self-authenticating. Thiemann, referring to a significant body of philosophical literature that argues against the possibility of non-inferential beliefs, finds Schleiermacher's attempts to establish such beliefs unconvincing. Schleiermacher must also justify the claim that the feeling of absolute dependence as an immediate non-inferential experience is a self-authenticating experience of God, and here, too, Thiemann concludes that Schleiermacher fails.

Revelation as "Divine Imposition"

Another notion of revelation as divine imposition, as Thiemann describes it, depends on a causal model of knowledge: knowledge can be imposed upon a subject by an object; in other words, the object causes the subject to know. In "a unique situation . . . human action is stilled and yet human beings become aware of or know God."[14] Thiemann refers to this as the "causal" model of revelation, not intending thereby to imply metaphysical causality, but merely intending to denote that the subject is caused to know (or has knowledge imposed upon it) by the object. His descriptive term "causal" is an epistemological one. Thiemann illustrates the notion of revelation as "divine imposition" with a quotation from Richard Rorty: "The notion of 'foundations of knowledge'—truths which are certain because of their causes rather than because of the arguments given for them—is the fruit of the Greek (and specifically Platonic) analogy between perceiving and knowing. The essential feature of the analogy is that knowing a proposition to be true is to be identified with being caused to do something by an object. The object which the proposition is about *imposes* the proposition's truth."[15]

A causal model of revelation, according to Thiemann, results from picturing the ontological otherness of God in spatial terms. For communication between God and humanity to occur, God must act upon that human realm which God transcends. While the autonomy of human action is granted in the realm of the ordinary, an extraordinary sphere has been created in which God is the supreme causal agent, and human beings are passive subjects or objects. The causal model implies that grace is a rare and extraordinary aspect of human life, while the everyday and ordinary are given over to autonomous human activity.

But why does Thiemann insist, as he does, that this causal model of revelation—which assumes an absolute contrast between faith and reason—is nonetheless foundationalist? In Thiemann's view, if revelation is causally imposed, and if the communication of revelation is not to be viewed as totally irrational, then the subjective side of the revelatory process can only be explained as intuition. And it is the supposed role that intuition plays in the process of coming to know that characterizes the supposed "foundations" of knowledge. With regard to those contemporary theologians who most obviously promote the notion of revelation as "divine imposition," or the causal model of revelation, Thiemann distinguishes two groups.

The first group of theologians bear close affinities to the thought of Søren Kierkegaard and the early writings of Karl Barth. Thiemann states that theologians in this group, in the twentieth century, have granted the category of revelation its most exalted status:

> These theologians are convinced that the prevenience of God's grace is not asserted forcefully enough in a position which begins from the assumption that God's revelation must be conformable to universal standards of rationality. In order to maintain the absolute

prevenience of grace, they argue, revelation must be conceived as that "impossible possibility" granted to the believer in a "moment of crisis." Revelation shatters the autonomous structure of human reason and communicates that which lies beyond reason's grasp. Theologians attracted to this crisis model begin from the conviction that the content of revelation, seen from the point of view of autonomous reason, is absolutely supra-rational. Nonetheless, God in his grace created in the human subject a capacity for receiving revelation through faith.[16]

Given a view of revelation as "that impossible possibility" granted to the believer in a "moment of crisis," whose content is absolutely supra-rational, the contrast between faith and reason could not be more stark. These theologians seem to revel in revelation's utter non-rationality. Theirs, according to Thiemann, is a classic Kierkegaardian understanding of revelation as "divine imposition."

A second set of theologians, according to Thiemann,

> accept the absolute contrast between revelation and autonomous reason [but] argue, nonetheless, that faith's grasp of revelation is reasonable. This argument requires both a criticism of the Enlightenment notion of reason's autonomy and an account of revelation's reasonableness which maintains the absolute prevenience of God's grace.
>
> Undoubtedly the most fully developed twentieth-century proposal of this sort comes in the work of the Scottish theologian Thomas Torrance.[17]

While the former group of theologians find revelation nonrational, the latter group, to which Torrance belongs, attempt to assert both the absolute uniqueness of revelation and the rationality of belief in it. They attempt to do so by denying the autonomy of human reason and giving precedence to the object's role in forming human knowledge. Torrance, for example, argues that the discipline of theology is rational and scientific in that it accepts the absolute primacy of its object of inquiry:

His argument for the reasonableness of revelation focuses on the rationality of the discipline of theology. Torrance poses this question: Can a discipline which accepts the absolute primacy of its object of inquiry be considered rational or scientific? Appealing to a model of rationality derived from the natural sciences he answers with a resounding "yes." In attending so carefully to its unique object theology exhibits the key characteristics of scientific objectivity—faithfulness to the nature of the object of inquiry and freedom from presuppositions foreign to its particular discipline.[18]

Because of these key characteristics, theology is a science, but it is a "special science." The object of theology is not a mute fact but a self-disclosing, self-communicating subject. The objects of other sciences "speak," that is, become understandable, only as they interact with the assumed concepts and categories of the science. For Torrance (still according to Thiemann), knowledge in other sciences emerges from the reciprocal interaction of object and schematizing subject; to some extent the object must be made to conform to the conceptual scheme if understanding is to occur. But this cannot be the case in theology. The schematizing process active in other sciences affects or controls the object that is known. This cannot occur in relation to God. Human subjectivity plays an essential but necessarily nonconstitutive role in the revelatory relationship. Knowledge of God arises from obedient conformity to God. All statements about God are God's statements and have their reference from a center in God and not in ourselves. Thus, rational interpretation in theology takes place only when we subordinate our subjectivity to God's objectivity and allow God to be the interpreter. Through its faithfulness to the divine nature of its object of inquiry and a freedom from irrelevant suppositions, theology is able to give precedence to the object's role in the formation of human knowledge. And it is able to do this while remaining fully rational.

For this second group of theologians, exemplified by Torrance—who take their cue from Kierkegaard insofar as they accept the absolute contrast between faith and reason—this reforming of human subjectivity to conform to revelation is what Thiemann terms "revelation as divine imposition." Thiemann's response is that if human subjectivity does not have a reciprocal effect on the divine object, then either the rationality of theology must be denied, or one must admit that the terms "knowledge" and "rationality" are being used equivocally. Thiemann points out that Torrance himself, in his criticism of Kant, acknowledges that a *reciprocal* relation between subject and object is a general characteristic of all rational inquiry. Torrance recognizes that knowledge results from the mind's interaction with that which is given to it. And Torrance affirms that "scientific knowledge must be evaluated in accordance with the prior structure of our consciousness," and that "the results of scientific knowledge are relative to the coercive devices we employ."[19] But for the knowledge that derives from revelation this cannot be the case.

In a passage from his *Theological Science*, Torrance states that only if the theologian thinks with the "inner compulsion" of God's self-revelation can theological concepts be adequate to their revealed object. Through that process the theologian finally gains "an intuitive apprehension of the whole pattern of Truth. . . . In natural science this is spoken of as *discovery*, in theology this is spoken of as *revelation*."[20] Passages such as this lead Thiemann to conclude that Torrance understands knowledge that derives from revelation to be "divinely imposed" or "causally imposed," while explaining the subjective side of this process in terms of "intuition." To the extent that Torrance makes this connection between "intuition" and causally imposed knowledge, he is committed, in Thiemann's view, to a form of theological foundationalism.

Thiemann summarizes the difficulty that he finds in Torrance's appeal to an intuitive or non-inferential knowledge of God as follows:

> His admittedly sophisticated and carefully argued position does not solve the problem of revelation but restates it in its sharpest form. . . . If we bring God into a context dominated by our categories and concepts, we treat him as if he were simply another object among the many objects we know through rational schematization. If we set God outside that framework and allow him to create his own conditions and content of knowledge, then we cannot say how it is that *we* know him. The former option denies God his divinity; the latter denies us our humanity.[21]

In Thiemann's view, therefore, Torrance's attempt to assert both the absolute uniqueness of revelation and the rationality of belief in it in the end collapses, and there is no way of overcoming its inconsistencies.

Epistemological Foundationalism

Thiemann traces the weakness that has beset religious epistemology in general back to John Locke, the founder of the modern discipline. According to Thiemann, "Locke clearly believes reason to be the central human faculty, 'Our last judge and guide in everything.'"[22] Yet Locke also states that revealed truths are "above reason."[23] Thiemann points out that faith, for Locke, might more accurately be categorized as "below reason," since it does not deal in true and certain knowledge.[24] In any case, for Locke, faith (the assent to any proposition on the grounds that it comes from God), though "above" reason, must be justified by an appeal to reason, and so it comes within reason's area of competence with regard to its justification. Thiemann thus identifies a tension in Locke's account of faith and reason. This tension is at the heart of Thiemann's complaint not merely against Locke's religious epistemology but against virtually every modern doctrine of revelation that has succeeded it. On the one hand, revealed truths are above reason or beyond knowledge; on the other, reason is the central human faculty, and faith, as a human reality, cannot exist except in connection with reason.

The tension that Thiemann identifies in Locke's account of faith and reason is crucial in relation to the epistemological difficulties that follow. It is *this* tension that has proved the stumbling block for the generations of theologians that have followed Locke. As Thiemann says, it has tended to result either in the view that revelation designates a special category of truths undergirded by a unique mode of knowing, or in the view that God can be known in the same way that a finite object may be known. Thiemann clearly thinks that Locke holds the former view.

Locke defines reason in contradistinction to faith:

> Reason . . . I take to be the discovery of the certainty or probability of such propositions or truths, which the mind arrives at by deduc-

tion made from such ideas which it has got by the use of its natural faculties, viz. by sensation or reflection. Faith, on the other side, is the assent to any proposition, not thus made out by the deductions of reason but upon the credit of the proposer as coming from God, in some extraordinary way of communication. This way of discovering truths to men we call revelation.[25]

For a Lockean, according to Thiemann, the truths of reason and the truths of revelation differ in three basic ways: "They stem from dissimilar sources (sense ideas versus God's 'extraordinary way of communication'); they are grasped by different mental processes (the deductions of reason versus accepting the credit of the proposer); and they elicit distinctive kinds of assent (certainty or probability versus mere assent)." Thiemann adds, "Reason cannot discover the truths of faith, nor justify them by deduction."[26]

According to Thiemann, as we have seen, theologians have often sought to validate revealed truths by an appeal to intuition, resulting in the incoherence of epistemological foundationalism. Epistemological foundationalism is the fundamental flaw that runs through modern doctrines of revelation. As Thiemann understands the term, foundationalism is the view that the "correspondence between the self-evident beliefs and the language independent world" is justified immediately by a form of direct experience or intuition.[27] Despite "his non-foundational Kierkegaardian starting point,"[28] Torrance's use of the term *intuition* to signify the absolute certainty of causally imposed knowledge, in Thiemann's view, commits even him to a form of foundationalism. In his consideration of Schleiermacher's theology, Thiemann objects to intuition because it seems to bypass the material world and is thought to be precognitive. In contrast, Torrance explicitly denies the validity of precognitive experiences.[29] Thiemann's objection to Torrance's version of intuition is not that Torrance treats it as precognitive, but that, being put forward as cognitive, he nonetheless presents it as bypassing the normal cognitive structures of the human being. Thus we should conclude that Torrance, like Schleiermacher, is not dealing with what is normally understood by knowledge.

Karl Rahner in his work *Hearer of the Word* similarly identifies two kinds of attempts by Protestant theologians to defend the rationality of belief. Like Thiemann, he argues that both approaches suffer from the same flaw, although he expresses the flaw differently:

> For the Protestant philosophers of religion (whether or not they go under this name) the content of religion, as expressed in doctrine, worship, and so on, may be interpreted in either of two ways. For the first group it is merely the objectivation of the religious conditions of the human subject, as an experience of value, or a feeling of utter dependence, or an awareness of justification, and so on. For the second group it is the word of the living God as it sovereignly judges all that is finite and human. The word is utterly unexpected. Compared with it all human reality appears as absolute darkness and contradiction, as mere kenosis of the God revealed in and through the godless shadows of everything finite. This is so true that God and this revelation turn properly into the dialectically necessary correlate of humanity's radical godlessness, and that basically nothing can be revealed except God's judgment over everything finite. Thus God is either the inner meaning of the world and of humanity and nothing more. Or God is the one who utterly contradicts us and our world.
>
> The first trend derives from Schleiermacher and Ritschl. . . . The second trend is that of the dialectical theology of Barth, Brunner, and their followers. Ultimately, however, these two trends converge into one. Revelation—insofar as this word is or may still be used—is simply something correlative to human nature itself. Only the signs differ. The first trend uses the plus sign: God is the meaning of humanity, nothing more. The other one employs the minus sign: God is the *No* addressed to humanity, nothing more.[30]

For Rahner the two types of argument reflect in complementary ways a single mistake common to both main strands of Protestant thought: that of treating God as the correlative of human nature. Thiemann takes the view that the mistake has been to think, in the first place, that it is possible to provide an epistemological account of revelation.

The Normal Means of Knowing

For Thiemann, as we have seen, attempts to demonstrate the reasonableness of faith in the truths of revelation have usually resulted in one of two views. On the first, God can be known in the same way that a finite object can be known through the normal means of knowing. This view, however, cannot properly accommodate the notion of God's transcendence. On the second, revelation designates a special category of truths undergirded by a unique mode of knowing that differs from the normal means of knowing. So what, in Thiemann's view, is the normal means of knowing? How does he understand "the normal structures of knowledge?"

Thiemann's own epistemology is difficult to establish since he does not explicitly admit to one, presumably because he understands his position to be "beyond" epistemology. However, he consistently implies a coherentist position. For example: "The distinction between inferential and non-inferential beliefs is difficult either to establish or overturn as a general distinction. One must simply analyze and evaluate the arguments and evidence brought forward in support of the more obscure category—the non-inferential beliefs." He follows this with a wholly negative evaluation of non-inferential beliefs.[31] He also refers in a note, as mentioned earlier, to "a significant collection of philosophical literature which argues against the possibility of non-inferential beliefs," beginning with the works of "the intellectual father of these arguments," Charles Peirce.[32] In his own arguments Thiemann in fact appears to adopt a strict coherence theory of knowledge, whether it be knowledge about God or knowledge about created reality. The normal means of knowing is through coherence, based on the process of inference.

Thiemann has identified the flaw common to both the liberal and the dialectical tradition as "epistemological foundationalism," that is, the view that there is "a set of non-inferential, self-evident beliefs which serve as the given or foundation of all knowledge." This involves a distinction between foundational beliefs, which are justified immediately by a form of direct experience or intuition, and propositions arrived at through inference. Theologians have sought to overcome the tension between the notions of reason and of revelation by an appeal to the notion of intuition.

And as Thiemann interprets this appeal, faith is connected to reason not by means of the normal processes of inference (which would imply that revealed truths could be brought within the sphere of reason) but by means of foundational beliefs which are intuited. "Intuition" is "incoherent," which for Thiemann means that it does not operate within the process of coherence that structures human knowledge. It is not based on inference.

His insistence on coherence allows for no intuitive apprehension. Intuition, for Thiemann, always occasions incoherence. It implies a direct access to ultimate reality, direct in the sense that it is not mediated by any created reality. Intuition would equate to the notion of an "intellectual" or "metaphysical" intuition, which Rahner, for instance, rejects in his *Spirit in the World*.[33] It would be a knowledge of metaphysical reality that occurs without the use of images; in other words, it would be a knowledge which is totally unmediated by the material world. In rejecting such a notion, Thiemann thereby rejects any role for correspondence in the process by which human understanding comes by what it knows. Thiemann believes that the only alternative to intuition is the coherence that derives from inferential reasoning.

Assuming that coherence is the normal means of knowing, the notion of correspondence, like the notion of intuition, also necessarily implies incoherence. Foundational beliefs supposedly correspond to a reality that is perceived to be independent of language. In Thiemann's view, they supposedly bypass the normal structures of knowledge and therefore also of language. Furthermore, correspondence always implies that knowledge is imposed. Thiemann includes in his definition of epistemological foundationalism the assertion that foundationalists understand the relationship between God and human beings as "causal," with God conceived as a "transcendent object";[34] characteristic of all foundational epistemologies is "the imposition of truth."[35] If certain truths bypass the normal processes by which a human being comes to know—if they are intuited—then they are imposed; they are impressed upon the human being in a way that bypasses the normal functioning of the cognitive structures of the mind. But if the "ordinary means of knowing" refers to Thiemann's coherence theory of knowledge, any supposed direct apprehension would not be part of the ordinary means of knowing. It would be intuitive, it would rely on the notion of correspondence, and it would constitute the imposition of truth. In other words, it would be incoherent.

Human Freedom

A correspondence theory of knowledge is, in Thiemann's view, not only incoherent but also involves a loss of human freedom. Thiemann in fact interprets the knowing of correspondence in terms of some sort of coercion or control, either on the part of the knowing subject over that which is known or vice versa: "the correspondence can be guaranteed only if the mechanism by which we know is causally determined and thus reliable. To know is thus to be compelled either by the reality of the object or by the invariant structure of the subject's consciousness. The ontological gap is then bridged either by the imposition of the object's nature upon the knowing subject or by the imposition of the subject's consciousness upon the un-schematized object."[36]

Running through Thiemann's analysis of the causal model of revelation is his concern for human freedom. The passivity of the human subject in the reception of revelation has implications for freedom:

> The causal model [of communication between God and humanity] has seemed especially relevant for the problem of revelation, because the cause and effect relation embodies the active-passive distinction necessary to preserve God's prevenience. . . . But while causation might well describe God's original act of creation, it is not clear that it is an apt notion either for an understanding of *creatio continua* or for conceiving of the process by which we become aware of our ultimate dependence upon God. To conceive either of the latter two relations under the notion of causation is to threaten the freedom which is an essential part of responsible human action.[37]

Whether revelation is impressed or imposed by God, the human mind does not engage in the schematizing process but remains passive. Even Torrance's version of "intuition" brings with it this problem, since intuition bypasses the normal cognitive structures of the human mind. The reason why many theologians have concluded that revelation must be imposed is not merely because revelation must be shown to be above reason and God's prevenience maintained; they are also concerned that there should be no corruption of the content of revelation, and no loss of the certainty that relevation guarantees.

Torrance, for example, wants to allow a role for human subjectivity in the process of revelation but cannot allow for any active intellectual involvement in it: "Torrance wants human subjects to be involved in the act of revelation; he simply does not want their reception of revelation to influence the absolute certainty of its content."[38] Torrance thus arrives at a theory whereby the object which the proposition is about imposes the proposition's truth. Human freedom, Thiemann responds, is then called into question, since the human being is treated as the passive recipient of self-evident truth.

Thiemann thus concludes that Torrance sacrifices freedom to ensure the certainty of the content of revelation. Interestingly, Thiemann's understanding of the relationship between freedom and certain knowledge echoes that of Swinburne. Swinburne identifies freedom with the choice whether or not to believe something—a choice that would be taken away if knowledge were certain. Furthermore, both Thiemann and Swinburne identify this freedom, which can only be exercised in the absence of certain knowledge, with the fundamental freedom to accept or reject God in faith, or the freedom to live out a life of faith. While Swinburne thinks that if human beings could be certain of God's existence they would lose their freedom to reject God, Thiemann thinks that the imposition of certainty regarding the content of revelation can be identified with the "imposition" of salvation. For Thiemann, there is a link between the certainty of God's revelation and problems having to do with predestination and the bondage of the human will.

The concerns of Thiemann and of Swinburne are undoubtedly expressed differently, based on their different understandings of human nature and of grace. Swinburne's emphasis is on human agency: the human being, having acquired faith, acts in such a way as to secure his or her own salvation. Thiemann's emphasis is on divine agency: God through grace secures the human being's salvation. God's gracious action consists in revelation. If revelation is imposed on some human beings, as the causal model of revelation implies (on Thiemann's account of it), then their free will would be compromised. Thiemann comments that "one reason the causative model has been attractive to some theologians is that it allows a continuation of an emphasis on predestination and/or the bondage of the will." Predestination is not an area that Thiemann wants to get into; he does not want his appeal "for freedom as a presupposition for responsible action to be understood as implying a position on freedom in relation to divine election."[39] Like Swinburne, however, Thiemann identifies freedom, as a presupposition for responsible action, with an absence of certainty regarding the content of revelation.

Thiemann's "Non-causal" Method

Thiemann's position is that attempts to demonstrate that claims to revelation are not contrary to reason and yet also to hold that revelation designates a special category of truths have resulted in a pervasive incoherence. As a result, Thiemann states, "knowledge of God" is itself "a problematical notion for theology."[40] Thiemann argues that accounts of knowing rely primarily on metaphors of sight, but it is impossible to determine whether eschatological knowing is rightly described on the model of seeing. In any case, to assert that our present knowledge somehow participates in that future knowing involves an appeal to a form of intuitive knowing—which, for Thiemann, is at the center of the conceptual confusion of foundationalism.

Thiemann's solution is to leave aside what he understands by epistemological questions. He allows that one may still speak in some sense of "knowledge of God," and therefore of revelation: that in which "the God identified in biblical narrative is trustworthy."[41] Revelation, however, should not be treated as a matter of epistemological inquiry. By moving the doctrine of revelation to an altogether different ground, Thiemann believes he can avoid becoming caught up in epistemological difficulties.

Thiemann therefore seeks to distance himself from the idea of revelation as an epistemological doctrine, and to recast the doctrine in such a way that it is no longer understood in terms of "God's knowability" in any ordinary sense of the word "knowability." "Knowability" for Thiemann seems to imply a congruence, which is achieved by force, between the human mind and the object. It implies control of one over the other, either on the part of the mind or on the part of the object that is known. Similarly, Thiemann seems to understand "causal" in terms of force or control. When the theology of revelation is understood as an investigation of God's knowability, it inevitably becomes an inquiry into the conditions of the possibility that God can be known, and known through some kind of power relationship. For Thiemann, a definition of revelation as an investigation into God's knowability "encourages a conception of the doctrine as an inquiry into the conditions of the possibility that God can be known, i.e., as a foundational transcendental enquiry."[42] "Transcendental" here means the "otherness" of God pictured spatially, in such a way that in the communication between God and humanity, God "causes" the human being to know.[43]

Thiemann proposes instead a very different approach to revelation. The alternative definition of the doctrine of revelation is "an account of God's identifiability."[44] Thiemann will *analyze* or *describe* the way in which God can be identified in Scripture, drawing on thinkers, notably David Kelsey and Charles Wood, who give a "functionalist" interpretation of Scripture. The advantage of functionalism, for Thiemann, is that it is "descriptive"—it *describes* the ways in which Scripture is actually used. To him the *description of function* offers a method of interpretation that avoids the foundationalism inherent in all the other interpretations that he has explored. It also offers a way to defend the doctrine of revelation without implying that revelation signifies control—either on the part of the mind or on the part of the object that is known. Since "knowability" implies control, Thiemann will assiduously avoid any reference to "knowability," "knowing" or "knowledge," as he sets out his defense. His method will be a *non-causal* one.

Thiemann's Functionalism

Rather than being "foundationalist" or "epistemological," therefore, Thiemann's defense of Christian faith is "functionalist" insofar as it describes the way in which the biblical text is *used*, rather than being concerned with its meaning. Thiemann rejects an epistemological doctrine of revelation, according to which Scripture is authoritative on account of its revealed content, and offers in its place a functional view of the authority of Scripture. Scripture is authoritative precisely because it functions authoritatively. The stress is on its use. Thiemann describes this as the "neo-Wittgensteinian option."[45] The function that Thiemann attributes to Scripture—or at least to the theological concepts that result from its use—is that of regulating the shared form of Christian life. The "normative" or regulative uses to which the scriptural texts are put are their primary function. In other words, like Lindbeck, Thiemann understands the main function of doctrines as regulative.

Thiemann, who is indebted to Hans Frei's account of the eclipse of biblical narrative, criticizes the way in which Christian claims about reality are often referred, in the first instance, to philosophical claims rather than directly to the biblical narrative. The meaningfulness of revelation has come to depend for many upon a prior religious context independent of the scriptural narratives, rather than being found within the scriptural narratives themselves. From David Kelsey, Thiemann takes the notion that Scripture must be construed as an imaginative whole, and from Charles Wood he takes the view that Scripture is best interpreted as a *narrative* whole. According to Kelsey, the precise manner in which Scripture functions authoritatively for theology will depend on the particular way in which the theologian construes the text as a whole. Even to call a set of texts "Scripture" is to "ascribe some kind of wholeness to it."[46] Ascribing wholeness results in "imaginative construals" which are "logically irreducibly diverse."[47] Theologians thus make a "decision" about what constitutes the subject matter of theology; this is determined by the way in which the theologian "tries to catch up what Christianity is basically all about in a single, synoptic, imaginative judgment."[48]

The imaginative construction placed on Scripture considered as a whole determines the precise way in which Scripture functions authoritatively for theology. Wood, for example, treats the canon of scripture (the sixty-six books of the Bible) as a *narrative* whole in the sense that all the books of the Bible should be read as one story, with God as its author.[49] This is the line that Thiemann adopts, quoting Wood: "It is a story in which real events and persons are depicted in a way that discloses their relationship to

God and to God's purposes; a story that finally involves and relates all persons and events, and which, as it is told and heard in the power of God's Spirit, becomes the vehicle of God's own definitive self-disclosure."[50]

For Thiemann the authority of Scripture is of paramount importance. Yet he seeks to replace the traditional way in which this authority has been understood with a new way. According to Thiemann, the modern doctrine of revelation, with its traditional understanding of scriptural authority, is systematically misleading because it implicitly denies the variety of ways theologians actually use Scripture. The standard Protestant doctrine of revelation teaches that Scripture should be understood as the "source" of "revealed content," and that authority should be defined as a quality of the scriptural text. Theology is then the translation of the Bible's revealed content. This version of theology, however, was based on what Thiemann and Wood regard as two false assumptions: that there is a single meaning to be discerned in a scriptural text, and that authority is an inherent quality of the text itself. The view that there is a single meaning to be discerned in any text is one that Wittgenstein in particular has called into question. According to the "neo-Wittgensteinian option," knowing has no universal shape, and there is no ultimate foundation of all knowledge. Since there is no single paradigm for all knowing, there is no single meaning to be discerned in a text. Again, quoting Wood:

> It is commonly asserted that the goal of interpretation is to understand the meaning of the text, as if "meaning" were the object of "understanding." . . . Implicit in the formula is the notion that meaning is a property of a text: the text means. But this is surely misleading. In correct usage, the phrase, "The text means . . ." is always elliptical. What the phrase obscures is the connection between the text and its user or users. . . . There is no escape from the issue of the text's uses, despite the illusory security of "the meaning of the text."[51]

If one asks for the use of a text rather than its meaning, Thiemann comments, one finds "not a singular object of understanding or a singular process but irreducible diversity."[52]

The second assumption, namely, that authority is an inherent quality of the scriptural texts, is also one that has been called into question by theologians such as Wood and Kelsey. While Scripture has been understood as the "source" of "revealed content," this is only one of several possible ways to conceive the relation between the Bible and theology. In Thiemann's view there are other and more apt ways of using Scripture and understanding its authority. Rather than defining the authority of Scripture as a quality of the text, Thiemann follows Kelsey in arguing for a "functional" definition of authority. According to this functional definition, the biblical text has no inherent authority of its own, but it becomes authoritative through the decision to take it as authoritative. To say that biblical texts are authoritative is simply "to say that they ought to be *used* in the common life of the church in normative ways such that they decisively rule its form of life and forms of speech."[53] Commenting on this last claim, which originates with Kelsey, Thiemann states:

> That claim indicates nothing about *how* they [the biblical texts] should so function or what particular patterns in scripture should rule Christian life and speech. It is a purely formal assertion. Kelsey emphasizes that conclusion by saying that the sentence "scripture is authoritative" functions as a "performative utterance." A theologian uttering the sentence indicates that he or she accepts the rule that scripture ought to norm theological proposals. All who accept that rule are playing the same theological "game," but they hold in common a purely formal understanding of scripture's role in theology.[54]

Thus to say that "scripture is authoritative" functions as a "performative utterance." Saying that it is authoritative renders it authoritative. Being authoritative, it may then be used to determine a Christian way of life and Christian forms of speech. Saying that it is authoritative of itself, however, gives no indication regarding what the Christian way of life and what the Christian forms of speech will be.

The theologian's task is first to construe the scriptural text as a whole, in order to make the texts usable as the norm for a way of life. The task is then to decide how, as the formal norm for a way of life, the text should be used in the material sense. The authoritative and regulative theological conceptualizations which result from the imaginative construal of Scripture as a whole will vary depending on the various imaginative construals of different theologians. These theological conceptualizations are what Lindbeck calls doctrines, and what in the Catholic tradition would be termed "dogma." It is these conceptualizations that determine the Christian way of life and Christian forms of speech.

Thiemann, however, goes beyond pure description of Scripture as an imaginative whole. In fact, he attempts to *justify* the notion that God is the author of the scriptural narrative—a justification which he attempts in terms of theological decisions. Thiemann holds that the depiction of God in the scriptural narrative requires justification. What is distinctive about Thiemann's account is the kind of justification he provides.

Thiemann admits that functional views of authority are theologically neutral: "their theological neutrality limits their usefulness in mounting a full-scale justification of belief in God's prevenience. In order to make a justificatory argument, a theologian must move beyond analysis to advocacy by offering reasons designed to persuade others that this belief is justified."[55] Thiemann intends to go beyond a purely analytic functionalism and offer "a defense of God's prevenience grounded, not in an epistemological account of the origin of Christian beliefs, but in an explication of the internal logic of that Christian conviction in relation to an understanding of scripture as a narrative depicting God's identity." This will not be "a general theoretical justification for belief in God's prevenience" but simply "some good reasons for affirming that belief, reasons which I hope will be convincing even to those who are not committed to the narrative image which lies at the center of my project."[56] He "will thus defend a modest doctrine of revelation," by which he simply means "an explication of the Christian conviction that the God identified in scriptural narrative truly issues his word of promise to the readers of the text."[57]

So far, Thiemann has asserted, first, that the theological significance of the text lies in the uses to which the text is put. Second, in order to be usable, the biblical texts must be construed imaginatively as a whole and the most useful controlling image is that of as a *narrative* whole. Third, the authority of Scripture lies in the fact that it is used in a normative, or regulative, way to mold the life and speech of the community. Finally, a theologian nevertheless must offer reasons designed to persuade others that belief in God's prevenience is justified. When we compare these four premises with Lindbeck's "cultural-linguistic" approach, we find that with respect to the first three, Thiemann and Lindbeck hold strikingly similar positions. Thiemann has departed from Lindbeck's position on the fourth. Lindbeck makes a nod to the correspondence theory of truth, but he regards justification as wholly inappropriate. Thus, while Lindbeck regards the challenge to Christian faith to provide some sort of evidence as inherently mistaken, Thiemann still accepts that some sort of evidence is needed.

Justification and Narrative Theology

Thiemann describes justification of Christian belief as dependent on "the coherent interrelations among Christian convictions concerning God's promises, their narrative enactment and fulfillment, and God's identity. That is to say that God's prevenience is logically linked to the truthfulness of the triune God's narrated promise."[58] Since God's revelation is not antecedent to the community's acceptance in faith—rather, the community's acceptance of revelation is the same thing as their interpretation of revelation—God's reality cannot be extrinsically related to Christian belief and practice. The relationship must be intrinsic. Accordingly, the "Christian claim to revelation asserts that God is identifiable 1) within the narrative as Yahweh who raised Jesus from the dead, 2) through the narrative as the God of promise who in addressing his promise to the reader is recognized as *pro nobis* and *extra nos,* and 3) beyond the narrative as the one who, faithful to his promises, will fulfill his pledge to those whom he loves." The paradigm of promise, rather than of knowledge, is central in conceiving God's relation to humanity.[59] Thiemann thus proposes a justification in terms of "promise" rather than in terms of propositional statements. His use of the notion of promise will become clear later in this chapter.

As we have seen, Thiemann's approach is a descriptive functionalism. It aims to illuminate the structures embedded in beliefs and practices and "to show the intelligibility, aptness and warranted assertability of Christian beliefs," but not to defend them theoretically. "Descriptive theology eschews theoretical defenses of Christian doctrine."[60]

The term "warranted assertability" originated with the philosopher John Dewey, who interpreted truth in terms of warranted assertability and in so doing seemed to assimilate truth with verification. Dewey called "warranted assertability" the evidence that moves one along toward the goal of inquiry, which is not some species of abstract truth but a "transformed situation."[61] Thiemann claims that he uses the term "warranted assertability," normally associated with pragmatism, to emphasize that his defense of Christian beliefs is nonfoundational. While he affirms the progressive character of justification, which means that even settled belief must be open to further inquiry, he also wants to argue that there are procedures for settling beliefs and justifying claims to truth. The concept of "warranted assertability," he says, "stands opposed to foundational theories of truth but not to the notion of justified true beliefs."[62]

In contrasting his own defense or justification with the flawed theoretical justification of epistemological foundationalism, Thiemann also uses the term "holist justification."[63] This consists "in seeking the relation between a disputed belief and the web of interrelated beliefs within which it rests."[64] To decide whether a belief should be considered normative is to ask whether it fits coherently with other beliefs of Christianity that are taken to be normative.

Having rejected the "causal model" of the relationship between God and human beings, Thiemann requires another model to defend the belief in God's "priority." Clearly God is not "spatially" other than them. Nor is God "temporally" prior to them. Thiemann refers in this connection to James Barr, who is concerned about the tendency of believers to identify revelation as an antecedent event to which faith is a subsequent response.[65] Barr asks, How can we speak about an antecedent revelation to which the scriptural witness is the response, when that response is itself the source of our knowledge of the antecedent revelation? While the community claims a distinction between the divine initiative and the response of faith, the contemporary interpreter has access to God's initiative only in the faith response, that is to say, only through the community's interpretation. In these circumstances one cannot distinguish revelation from the faith of the community. Rather than seek to establish God's temporal priority, descriptive theology seeks to establish that God's reality and thus God's "ontological" priority are implied by a set of concrete Christian beliefs concerning God's identity. Revelation is then "the continuing reality of God's active presence among his people."[66]

Thiemann finds a deeper issue implied in Barr's challenge: whether we can speak of God's priority in any sense, if the only basis for theological claims is the faith and tradition of the Christian community. The claims of the original community who claimed to receive God's revelation seem to be "self-referential." A self-referential claim is one that claims something about itself; in this case, that it has received God's revelation. If the relation between Christian claims and God's reality is extrinsic (that is, if God is an external, causal agent), then self-referential claims cannot be claims about God because God, according to this view, is an external reality who consequently stands outside all human language. Therefore Christian claims, or the claims of the Church's faith, can imply nothing about this God. Conversely, if Christian claims about God are true, then God's reality cannot be extrinsically related to Christian belief and practice. Rather, the relationship must be intrinsic. In Thiemann's words, "the report about God's reconciliation cannot be separated from the good news itself, because the gospel is the *report* of God's reconciliation, the present *gift* of that reconciliation, and the *promise* of the future triumph of God's reconciling action."[67]

Once it has been established that God's reality is intrinsically, not extrinsically, related to Christian belief and practice, it is the narrative shape of the biblical materials that enables the depiction of the personal identity of God, and hence the identification of God as prevenient. "Narrative" is itself a term open to dispute. Thiemann finds that some theologians regard narrative primarily as a transcendental quality of experience, or a universal form of consciousness. This implies a view of theology very much like the foundational theology Thiemann criticizes. It regards the primary theological task as the construction of a philosophical anthropology—a transcendental view of human being and language—and the correlation of Christian concepts with those transcendental categories. This use of narrative continues the "turn to the subject" which has dominated theology since Kant. Other theologians regard narrative as a literary form, which should be interpreted according to appropriate literary techniques. Of the two, Thiemann is attracted to this second idea of narrative and the idea that the category of narrative becomes a useful tool for the interpretation of Scripture. Narrative highlights both a predominant literary category within the Bible and an appropriate theological category for interpreting the canon as a whole. Narrative as a theological category provides an organizing image for a theology concerned to reassert the primacy of God's personal identity.

The concept of narrative is useful in the reassertion of God's prevenience by a nonfoundational theology because it provides a coherent theological alternative to theologies focused on the primacy of philosophical anthropology. It provides a way of construing the canon as whole, which integrates the first-order language of Scripture and the second-order description of theology. It is able to integrate a central literary genre in Scripture with an organizing theological image. In spite of the "irreducible diversity" of the integral narratives found in Scripture, there are ample reasons for literary critics and theologians to believe that a form of narrative unity, governed by the shape of the text itself, can be discovered within the diverse material of the canon. Narrative also focuses attention on the centrality of God's agency within biblical narrative and Christian community. Characterization is an important element of narrative structure. As we see characters act and suffer within the framework of the plot, we come to know and understand them. Narratives present patterns of characteristic action, which depict personal identity. The theologian can speak of God's intentions as enacted in the actions of Israel and Jesus. Scripture's "main character" is God, and yet God's direct actions are only rarely described. God's agency is most often depicted through the description of acts of other agents, that is to say, through the agency of the people of Israel and of Jesus. Those acts which occur through human agents are, insofar as they move toward a *telos* retrospectively discerned, the very acts of God. The indirectness of Scripture's depiction of God's agency allows an affirmation of God's hiddenness.

Thiemann contrasts the historical setting of Scripture with the end of the world which is still to come, and concludes with an affirmation of God's hiddenness. This is reminiscent of Wolfhart Pannenberg, who says that "only in connection with the end of the world that still remains to come can what has happened in Jesus through his resurrection from the dead possess and retain the character of revelation for us also."[68] Thiemann seems to overcome the Protestant reticence with regard to defending the doctrine of revelation by qualifying the notion of revelation with a reference to the future.

Truth-Claims

Given that Christian truth-claims cannot be justified by non-inferential self-evident arguments, Thiemann considers that it is nonetheless still possible to "make historical or ontological claims to truth."[69] Christian faith demands this: while there is no natural or innate connection between human language and God's reality, faith demands that "once God has claimed a piece of creaturely reality as his own and bound himself to it, then we are warranted in accepting the God-forged link between the human and divine."[70] On the basis of Philipp Melanchthon's interpretation of the term "promise," Thiemann argues in some detail that God has taken over the language of promise as a vehicle for self-disclosure. And since promise is the vehicle for God's self-disclosure, Christian truth-claims may be justified if the one who makes the promise can be identified as trustworthy. The Christian claim to truth depends on

> whether Christians are warranted in believing God's promises to be true. Since these truth-claims take the form of promises, their justification has an inevitable prospective or eschatological dimension. The justifiability of one's trust in the truthfulness of a promise is never fully confirmed (or disconfirmed) until the promiser actually fulfills (or fails to fulfill) his/her promise. Until the time of fulfillment the promisee must justify trust on the basis of a judgment concerning the character of the promiser. It is justifiable to trust a promiser if his/her behavior on balance warrants that trust. Thus investigation into warranted assertability must examine the identity of the promiser, the nature and context of the promises, and the demands made of those who await their fulfillment. It is only in the context of that relationship that Christian claims to truth can be justified.[71]

Christian truth-claims may be justified only within the relationship between God and those to whom God has made promises, and only on the basis of trust. That trust is justified on the basis of whether God's behavior, as discerned in Scripture, *on balance* warrants that trust.

It is interesting to note here that Thiemann, like Swinburne, deals in some sense with the "balance" of probability. It is also significant that Swinburne, who tries to meet directly the challenge to give evidence for religious belief, holds that the judgment regarding the balance of probability is one that can be made by anyone. In contrast, Thiemann, who tries to meet the challenge based on the mediation of knowledge, holds that the judgment regarding the balance of probability can be made only by those who are already part of the Christian narrative.

The above demonstrates how heavily Thiemann's account relies on the notion of "promise." Thiemann has given the justification of truth a future reference. In so doing, he brings his thinking back in line with the Lutheran tradition and avoids a justification based on what can be known *now*.

The Justification of God's Trustworthiness

Thiemann sets out to demonstrate God's trustworthiness by making a distinction between the "locutionary act" and the "illocutionary act—a distinction he borrows from J. L. Austin.[72] In any given sentence the locutionary act can be identified by the sentence's propositional content, but the illocutionary act can be identified only by the particular context within which the speech-act is performed. In the act of speaking we communicate both through the propositional content of our speech and through the context in which it is spoken. Thiemann refers to that which is communicated through the context as "the 'force' which that speech possesses in a particular linguistic context."[73]

Thiemann analyzes the "force" and the "propositional content" of the Eucharistic Prayer. The propositional content clearly requires the logically prior belief in God's prevenience. The "force" of the Eucharistic Prayer also presupposes God's prevenience. The activities of worship—adoration, confession, thanksgiving, and supplication—are the Church's response to God's initiative and action. The "propositional content" further specifies the web of beliefs within which the belief in God's prevenience rests.

> God is identified primarily as the *God of promise* whose promises receive *narrative enactment and fulfillment* in the history of Israel and the life, death and resurrection of Jesus. God's identity is further specified by the *triune structure* of the Eucharistic Prayer. It is addressed to the Father, God of creation and promise; it narrates the actions of the Son which extend and fulfill the Father's promises; and it invokes the gift of the Spirit, the presence of God among the gathered faithful and the pledge of God's consummate fulfillment of all his promises. That triune structure is replicated in the prayer's description of the church as that community which remembers the story of God's saving acts, trusts in God's continued faithfulness to his promises, and hopes for his final return in power.[74]

In the Gospel of Matthew, as Thiemann points out, Jesus' final act of promising extends the Gospel's promise "to the whole world." Jesus, whose identity is depicted in the Gospel's narrative, now becomes the agent of promise as the story becomes a proclamation addressed to the reader. Matthew (in chapter 28) creates "narrative space" for his readers within the Gospel story,

> by explicitly reminding them that the fellowship of the disciples has been reduced in number.... Thus the opportunity remains for the reader to join the company of disciples by responding in faith and undertaking the journey of discipleship.
>
> By refusing to provide premature closure for his story, Matthew allows the narrative discourse to flow from the text to the reader. The reader who responds in faith is incorporated into the world of the narrative, and the story continues through the community created by this narrated promise. Precisely as the narrative provides its definitive identification of God and Jesus, it also functions as a promise of direct address. In narrating the story of God's promise, the Gospel identifies Jesus as the one in whom God's intentions are

enacted, and so addresses that narrated promise to the reader. Thus the discourse . . . functions between the text and the reader as an invitation to enter the world of the text."[75]

The reader who responds in faith to the narrative is incorporated into the world of narrative, and the story continues through the community created by this narrated promise. God's prevenience is established not only as an intelligible category within the discourse of the text, but also as a reality which confronts the reader through the text. It accounts both for God's relation to and God's priority within our framework of belief. God's prior initiative must be distinguished from the response of the community of faith. The promises of God depicted within the text become his promise to those who stand outside the text. The reader is offered the opportunity to make a judgment concerning the reality of the God who invites and the truth of the promises issued.

In order to respond to this invitation, the reader must recognize this narrative as God's personal promising address. "To recognize the gospel as God's personal address the reader must further acknowledge that God is an existent promising agent in actual communication with the human recipient. A correlative response of faith and discipleship indicates that the hearer recognizes both the *extra nos* and *pro me* character of God's narrated promise."[76]

The event that establishes both God's identity and the narrative's promissory function is Jesus' resurrection. "When God is identified as God of promise, and the biblical narrative as his promissory address, then the reader is invited to respond in faith and discipleship. If the reader does so respond, a context of interpretation is created in which the content and force of the text are logically prior to the correlative response."[77] Thiemann seems to mean that both the propositional content of the biblical narrative, and that which is communicated through the narrative's context, are prior to the reader's response. Thus the context for God's utterance flows from the text to the reader. Promise and promiser must precede response. Context (the context in which it is read) normally functions to control interpretation, but biblical narrative should be excepted from this general rule "because the structure and content of these texts suggest a reverse hermeneutical procedure for their interpretation."[78] Their narrative content, that is, their identification of God, becomes decisive for the correlative response. The Christian has no way to explain how this "reverse hermeneutical procedure" occurs. The content of biblical narrative thus gives rise to a distinctive hermeneutical situation within the Christian community. This revised account of revelation provides a way to distinguish God's initiative from faith's response.

God's priority is not solely a matter of semiotic relations within the biblical narrative. Christians are warranted in asserting that the biblical narrative serves as God's promising address to those who stand outside the text as well. The text's narrative content has the "illocutionary force" of issuing the promise of salvation precisely as it describes God's identity in Jesus Christ. Faith is a response to the God who issues the promise, and who alone establishes the possibility of the act of communication. God's *extra nos* reality, as the existent God who issues a promise to the reader through the text, is recognized precisely as the *pro nobis* character of God's reality is acknowledged. Thus God's priority, and God's relation to human faith and intellect, are appropriately conceived when revelation is understood as God's narrated promise.

The Epistemological Value of "Recognition"

Thiemann, as we have seen, believes that a defense of the doctrine of revelation is essential to the survival of the Christian faith, and at the same time analyzes epistemological foundationalism as the root cause of incoherence in modern doctrines of revelation. He accepts the challenge that all human knowing, including knowledge of God, is mediated by the created world. He has sought to opt out of epistemology, yet still holds that talk of knowledge of God can be justified. And, as we have seen, he has attempted a justification based on a combination of two ideas—holism and promise. An objection that can be raised, however, is that as Thiemann interprets these two ideas, they turn out to be mutually contradictory.

Thiemann's version of holist justification equates truth with coherence. As noted above, he claims that "holist justification consists . . . in seeking the relation between a disputed belief and the web of interrelated beliefs within which it rests." Yet, on the basis of God's promise, Thiemann also offers a version of justification according to which God has taken over the language of promise as a vehicle for self-disclosure. While the holist justification relies on a coherence that occurs historically, the justification based on God's promise has an eschatological reference and relies on trust. These two versions of justification are not merely different; they are mutually incompatible. We have also seen that, in spite of its evident difficulties, Thiemann intends to take up Wood's overall vision of Scripture as a narrative whole with God as its author—a vision that is clearly foundationalist. One must conclude that Thiemann's defense of God's prevenience is confused or incoherent, and ultimately (with respect to Scripture) is a version of the very foundationalism that he criticizes.

What is evident immediately is that, despite Thiemann's intention to opt out of epistemology, his own Christian-specific argument is not epistemologically neutral. We have seen that he maintains a particular epistemological position—coherentist in character and opposed to foundationalism—which has a direct bearing on his understanding of what it means to know God. Indeed, what distinguishes his argument from opposing views is not Christian-specific but generally epistemological.

The essence of Thiemann's justification of knowledge of God is as follows: If God's prevenience is to be defended, then it is necessary to defend the doctrine of revelation. In order to defend revelation, Thiemann borrows principally from "functionalism" to propose a descriptive theology. Central to this descriptive theology is the category of narrative. Within the biblical narrative God is identified as the God of promise. According to Thiemann's argument, the God of promise of this narrative identification is necessarily "prevenient." Thiemann maintains that through the text, God's prevenience confronts the reader as a reality. This claim is based on a distinction, which Thiemann makes, between the "locutionary" element or "content" of what is spoken and the "illocutionary" element of speech. The latter includes a reference to context. Thus, according to the "illocutionary force" of the biblical texts, God's promise is addressed to the reader. In order to respond the reader must recognize the narrative as God's personal promising address. A response of faith and discipleship indicates that the hearer recognizes both the *extra nos* and the *pro me* character of God's narrative promise.

Thus Thiemann's defense of God's prevenience hinges on "recognition." The reader/hearer recognizes God's personal address—God's promise—and recognizes its *extra nos* and *pro me* character. Through this "recognition" one is confronted with God's prevenience as a reality. Thiemann explains this in his discussion of the Gospel of Matthew. Having borrowed from Austin the terms "locutionary act" and "illocutionary act," Thiemann also introduces a term borrowed from Paul Ricoeur: the "interlocutionary act," by which he means "a successful act of communication which elicits an appropriate response from the addressee."[79]

> Stated in terms of our analysis of the Gospel of Matthew: the biblical narrative's identification of God as the one who fulfills and renews his promise in raising Jesus from the dead suggests that the story's primary illocutionary force is that of promising. That promise serves further as an address to the Gospel's readers, inviting the response of faith and discipleship. In that interlocutionary situation of address and response the reader is offered the opportunity to make a judgement concerning the reality of the God who invites and the truth of the promises he issues. Thus questions of truth and reference arise in the interlocutionary context. In order to respond to this invitation the reader must *recognize* this narrative as God's personal promising address....
>
> While the structure and content of biblical narratives invite a *recognition* of the gospel's claims to truth, those claims are hardly *self-evident* implications of the text. Thus the text does not *compel* the reader to acknowledge the narrative as God's personal address.[80]

To discover the epistemology underlying Thiemann's defense of the doctrine of revelation, it is necessary to ask, what is the epistemological value of this "recognition"? Is recognition a matter of a new experience being synthesized with, or deduced from, previous experience? Or is recognition rather a direct, immediate, intuitive occurrence? According to Thiemann's own account of the "ordinary means of knowing," any supposed immediate experience, not depending on the process of inference, could not supply knowledge. Yet "recognition" does not seem to depend on a process of inference, and according to Thiemann's account it is precisely through a particular "recognition" that one comes to knowledge of God.

To say that this recognition of God's address takes place immediately, directly, and intuitively would be to set out the very understanding of revelation which Thiemann finds conceptually confused. Yet one could argue that recognition itself is inherently immediate, direct, and intuitive. To recognize something is to "see" it in a way that perhaps another person, or oneself on another occasion, faced with the same evidence and circumstances, does not "see" in that way at all. On the other hand, there may be something intuitive, in an everyday sense, about recognition, but there is no implication in the everyday sense that the subjective processes have been bypassed. Recognition may not be intuition in the strict sense in which Thiemann uses it. The difficulty, however, is one that Thiemann has made for himself. According to his own argument, unless recognition depends on the process of inference, it is automatically "intuitive" in the unacceptable sense and therefore incoherent. It cannot lead to knowledge.

We have already seen the significance of Thiemann's comment to the effect that Torrance's Kierkegaardian starting point is nonfoundational. The reason that Thiemann's limited attempt at justification fails is that his religious epistemology has as its fundamental premise the absolute contrast between faith and reason. Yet he finds himself compelled to attempt a limited justification of the belief fundamental to this theology—the notion of God's prevenience. Such justification, given his basic premise, is impossible.

As Thiemann has set up the problem, there is no alternative between "epistemological foundationalism," according to which a person would seem to bypass the material world in the process of coming to knowledge, and the coherentism which he favors, yet which he cannot adjust to make allowance for the Christian claim to truth. At this point Thiemann finds himself forced to do violence to his own epistemology. Having consistently stressed the priority of use over meaning in the interpretation of the scriptural text, he now advocates a "reverse hermeneutical procedure." Referring still to the recognition of the scriptural narrative as God's personal promising address, he maintains that once this recognition has taken place, a context of interpretation is created in which God's utterance flows from the text to the reader. Thiemann thus reverses his earlier position that the context (in which the text is read) functions to control interpretation. This "reverse hermeneutical procedure," as we saw, cannot be explained. "The Christian possesses no *theory to explain how* this reverse procedure occurs. All theology can do is describe the characteristics of biblical narrative and the correlative qualities of Christian discipleship which together constitute an interlocutionary relation in which priority is given to the promiser and his promise."[81]

Thiemann had argued that we should look for "use" rather than "meaning" in Scripture. By "use" he means the way in which those who use Scripture form their outlook and live their lives. He now argues in the reverse: prior to the way in which the text is used, the Christian is concerned with the propositional content of the biblical narrative and that which is communicated through the narrative's context. The content and "force" of the text are prior to, and exist independently from, the way in which the text is used. Ultimately, therefore, Thiemann treats reference and verifiability in terms of a form of independent reality—the content and "force" of the text. Despite his strictures against foundationalism, he is—at least if one accepts his own definition of the term—a foundationalist.

CHAPTER 4

Schleiermacher and Absolute Dependence

Michael J. Buckley in *At the Origins of Modern Atheism* has argued convincingly that a gradual separation of natural theology from metaphysics occurred beginning in the seventeenth century, with the rise of modern science and defenders of theism such as Lessing, Mersenne, and Descartes. For many ancient and medieval philosophers, there were questions about why anything whatsoever existed, questions about the "why" of being itself, which pointed to a completely "other" and transcendent cause. This metaphysical concept of a "first" cause was distinct from the concept of efficient causes or, by contrast, "second" causes. Efficient causality was by no means assumed to be the only possible form of causality or the only possible way of interpreting the dependent relation between a creature and that which explains the existence of any creature.

With the gradual abandonment of the older concept of an ultimate first cause, as traced by Buckley, the Christian God became portrayed as one cause among others. God was not totally other than the natural world. Rather, God and nature were parts of a larger whole. God became part of the system, an efficient, external cause of other data. Hand in hand with this went the idea that the human mind could investigate God rationally as one object of knowledge among others. The knowing subject was central. Deists defended God's existence in terms of "natural theology." The defense of the existence of God became independent of metaphysics as it was understood by most of the Scholastics. One might even say that with the collapse of the older concept and of its distinction of first from second causes, the distinction between infinite and finite also collapsed.

A central failing common to the theologies of both Swinburne and Thiemann has been identified in the earlier chapters. For all the obvious differences between them, each fails to do sufficient justice to the *distinction* between God and finite realities and between knowledge of God and knowledge of finite realities. Since God cannot be known in the way in which a finite object is known, human knowledge of God must be radically distinct from knowledge of the finite. Yet Swinburne and Thiemann each present a defense of Christian faith in which the divine and the human are depicted as the same *kind* of reality. Despite their efforts to respect the notion of God's transcendence, ultimately both are unable to incorporate into their account of the God/human relationship a recognition of the *infinite difference* between the transcendent and the transcended.

Yet since all human knowledge is mediated by the finite, knowledge of God must nevertheless be somehow dependent upon knowledge of finite realities. Human knowledge of God and human knowledge of finite realities, therefore, are correctly understood as radically distinct and yet mutually dependent. This distinction in mutual dependence must be the central component of any religious epistemology that reflects accurately the relationship between God and the world. What are the features that must characterize such an epistemology? Most obviously, it must recognize that *knowledge of God is mediated by the finite.* What else? We have seen that any suggestion that knowledge of God is somehow episodic, confined to particular experiences or particular factors given in experience, cannot do justice to the radical metaphysical difference between God and finite reality. A sound epistemology must, therefore, entail the notion that *knowledge of God is a permanent accompaniment to all human experience;* yet God and the world cannot be treated as parallel realities. Nor can God be treated merely as the substantive explanation for the existence of the world, or as the efficient cause of particular existents. Rather, as Buckley argues, a sound religious epistemology must uphold the metaphysical distinction between first and second causes.

Swinburne and Thiemann, admittedly in different ways, insist on the connections between knowledge of God and knowledge of finite reality:

Thiemann's polemic against foundationalist intuitions is matched by Swinburne's dismissal of a fideist appeal. Yet they both fail in their efforts to articulate the radical, indeed infinite, difference between the divine and the created. The question with which we are left is whether it is possible to articulate the connections in ways that nevertheless allow us adequately to honor the otherness, or the transcendence, of God. This is the task confronting those who believe that a sound religious epistemology is crucial to Christian apologetics. The remainder of this book is devoted to making the case that two theologians in particular, Friedrich Schleiermacher and Karl Rahner, can be of assistance in this task.

For all their underlying differences, Schleiermacher and Rahner have a certain common understanding of the relationship between God and the world. The study of Schleiermacher's theology in this chapter and of Rahner's theology in the following chapter investigate their common understanding of the God-world relationship and its bearing on epistemological matters. Both theologians have been much criticized precisely with regard to the sorts of issues that are the subject of this work, and thus certain criticisms regarding these issues are also addressed.

For the discussion of Schleiermacher it will suffice to refer to his two main works. The first is *On Religion: Speeches to Its Cultured Despisers*, corresponding to the original German edition *Über die Religion* of 1799 and referred to here as *Speeches*.[1] *Über die Religion* has dominated German study of Schleiermacher's early thought.[2] The second work is *The Christian Faith*, corresponding to the second edition of *Der christliche Glaube* (1830/1831).[3] Certain differences between the 1830/1831 edition and the first edition of 1821/1822[4] are also pertinent to the discussion (there is no English translation of the first edition).

The Neo-orthodox Criticism of Schleiermacher

Widely acknowledged within his own tradition as the most influential thinker since Calvin,[5] Schleiermacher nonetheless tends to be regarded as suspect by the generality of Protestant scholars, though there are some notable exceptions.[6] The most aggressive attack on Schleiermacher's work came from Emil Brunner, who in *Die Mystik und das Wort*[7] freely attributed to Schleiermacher, as the originator of liberal theology, whatever was to be found most objectionable in the Protestantism of the nineteenth century. Again, in his *Der Mittler,* translated into English as *The Mediator,* one can find any number of the unsubstantiated general criticisms of Schleiermacher to which both Brunner and Karl Barth were prone.[8] The subsequent dominance of neo-orthodoxy served largely to obscure Schleiermacher's actual teaching, since few theologians in the last century looked beyond the neo-orthodox travesty of Schleiermacher's position to discover Schleiermacher himself.

The other obstacle to an appreciation of Schleiermacher lies in his early links to Romanticism. Schleiermacher's association with the Romantic movement renders his theology both inspirational (even beautiful) and suspect. Two paintings by the German Romantic painter Casper David Friedrich (1774–1840), which seem to capture the mood that Schleiermacher evokes, provide an illustration of both the beauty and the potential danger of Romanticism. Friedrich's "Monk by the Sea" depicts a tiny robed figure looking out over dark, threatening waters and a huge expanse of mostly dark sky, with the merest hint of blue sky and sunlight beyond. His "Winter Landscape" depicts a group of fir trees in the snow, a mountain slope, and at a distance, shrouded in dark winter mist, the solid stone edifice of a church building. Closer inspection reveals a tall crucifix among the fir trees and a suppliant cripple leaning against an ice-covered rock at the foot of the cross, his crutches discarded in the snow. In the absence of any comment by Friedrich on these works, these pictures are, of course, open to different interpretations. Is God revealed to the monk through the mediation of the sea and the sky, or is the monk merely worshipping nature? Is the monk in the presence of God? Or does he simply project his own needs onto his surroundings and so create from his own intellectual resources the illusion of "God?" What is the relationship of the lame person to the institutional Church, represented by the edifice of the church? Is the Church with its doctrines relevant to his situation, or not? And how should we understand the crucified figure among the fir trees? As God from God, Light from Light, true God from true God—*homoousios* (of one substance) with the Father? Or merely as the perfect moral exemplar, a figure who as such arouses our deepest human emotions and moves us to a profound devotion? The influence of the Romantic movement on Schleiermacher implies that these sorts of questions must also be asked of him.

Schleiermacher and Transcendental Theology

On a superficial reading of his theology, Schleiermacher seems to be on a collision course with Rahner. Rahner's theology belongs within the movement known as transcendental Thomism and is heavily dependent on Thomist metaphysics. Schleiermacher, on the other hand, has an ostensibly negative attitude toward any sort of transcendental or metaphysical undertaking. He explicitly rejects "transcendental philosophy," which he equates with "metaphysics" under another name. Schleiermacher challenges the intended audience for his famous speeches, the "cultured despisers of religion," demanding to know, "What does your metaphysics do—or, if you want to have nothing to do with the outmoded name that is too historical for you, your transcendental philosophy?"—only to supply the answer himself in the form of an accusation: "It classifies the universe and divides it into this being and that, seeks out the reasons for what exists, and deduces the necessity of what is real while spinning the reality of the world and its laws out of itself."[9]

Yet Schleiermacher's own theology can legitimately be described as transcendental or metaphysical. On a closer reading it becomes apparent that Schleiermacher is not inherently hostile to a transcendental philosophy as such, but rather opposes the subjective idealism that, as he saw it, was having a disastrous impact on the religious thinking of his day. This he terms "transcendental." A contemporary of Fichte and Hegel, Schleiermacher bases his theology on the firm conviction that piety, rather than speculative theology, is at the center of true religion. His criticism is largely a polemic against the newest wave of "transcendental philosophy," which Schleiermacher associates with Fichte's *Science of Knowledge* (1794). Indeed, Schleiermacher expounds his position in contrast to the version of transcendental philosophy characterized by Fichtean dialectic. The target of Schleiermacher's polemic is a system, as in the quotation above, that spins "the reality of the world and its laws *out of itself*" (emphasis mine). Schleiermacher objects to the subjective idealism that he detects in Fichte, which will culminate in Hegel's philosophical idealism.

Schleiermacher followed Kant in refusing to countenance the possibility of a straightforwardly rational knowledge of God. Yet he rejected the Kantian view that religious faith could be reduced to the realm of practical reason. He also rejected any form of metaphysics that put the thinking subject at the structuring center of the act of knowing, in such a way as to imply that the human intellect was capable of bringing the whole of reality within its area of competence. Neither ethics nor a metaphysics that presumed to determine the nature of reality could be identified with religion. Religion was not a matter of "doing" or "knowing" in accordance with an autonomous system of moral laws or an autonomous system of the laws of philosophy. Whether the emphasis is on philosophy with some ethical input or on ethics with some philosophical input, those academics who expound the implications of subjective idealism and think that their findings can supplant religion, according to Schleiermacher, will simply destroy it.

> The theorists in religion, who aim at knowledge of the nature of the universe and a highest being whose work it is, are metaphysicians, but also discreet enough not to disdain some morality. The practical people, to whom the will of God is the primary thing, are moralists, but a little in the style of metaphysics. You take the idea of the good and carry it into metaphysics as the natural law of an unlimited and plenteous being, and you take the idea of a primal being from metaphysics and carry it into morality so that this might be engraved at the front of so splendid a code. But mix and stir as you will, these never go together; you play an empty game with materials that are not suited to each other. You always retain only metaphysics and morals. This mixture of opinions about the highest being or the world and of precepts for a human life (or even for two) you call religion![10]

Fichte was at the forefront of Schleiermacher's mind when he launched such attacks. It was not Fichte's supposed atheism that troubled Schleiermacher (Fichte was dismissed for atheism from his Chair of Philosophy at Jena in 1799). Rather, it was the fact that Fichte ventured even further than Kant in suggesting that practical reason determines theoretical reason. Fichte's system of transcendental idealism equates "God" with the supreme idea of moral duty, with the result that religion is subsumed under morality.

A rejection of the type of speculative or transcendental philosophy associated with Fichte's development of Kantian ethics characterizes all of Schleiermacher's theology. His *The Christian Faith* is written for the benefit of future preachers rather than cultured despisers of religion, and here the readers are constantly warned against mistaking speculative philosophy for dogmatics. Dogmatics is the science of faith, and must not be equated with metaphysics. Dogmatic propositions cannot derive from speculative philosophy—they cannot depend on any particular school of philosophy. "The Evangelical (Protestant) Church in particular is unanimous in feeling that the distinctive form of its dogmatic propositions does not depend on any form or school of philosophy, and has not proceeded at all from a speculative interest, but simply from the interest of satisfying the immediate self-consciousness solely through the means ordained by Christ, in their genuine and uncorrupted form."[11] Schleiermacher complains that the church is still very far from deriving its dogmatic propositions from faith in Jesus Christ, because "people take pains to base or deduce dogmatic propositions in the speculative manner."[12] The deduction from speculative thought of propositions relating to the divine ignores the limitations, the absolute dependency, of the human being in relation to God. It ignores the fact that faith is a divine and not a human work, and it should not presume to call itself religion.

Nonetheless, in spite of his implacable opposition to the speculative philosophy built upon Kant, Schleiermacher in his main systematic work, *The Christian Faith*, revises rather than rejects Kant's transcendental philosophy.[13] While denying that Kantian restrictions on reason can be placed on religion, Schleiermacher accepts the restrictions that Kant places on the scope of reason insofar as he accepts that reason can deal only with the sensible world. In opposition to Kant, however, Schleiermacher maintains that religious faith cannot be confined to the realm of practical reason, to the realm of ethics and morals. Religion deals with the "infinite" and cannot possibly be restricted to the finite realm; rather, it encompasses the finite realm. Schleiermacher thus follows Kant in positing a transcendental realm beyond the reach of reason, and by claiming that theology has to do with the realm beyond the finite, Schleiermacher engages in a kind of transcendental theology. The essence of religion, which is the immediate self-consciousness, has to do with the divine. It cannot be bound by the limitations of reason. It cannot be confined to the relationship between subject and object that is found in knowledge and action. In moving beyond the realm of reason, Schleiermacher concerns himself with the transcendent.

This description of Schleiermacher's work as a revision of Kant's transcendental philosophy could also be taken as a description of Rahner's project. In spite of Schleiermacher's explicit objections to "transcendental" theology, Schleiermacher and Rahner, as we will see, are close on this issue.

God, the Human Being, and Redemption

The key to both Schleiermacher's philosophical understanding of God and to his anthropology is his notion of piety (*Frömmigkeit*). Running through his work, from the *Speeches* to the two editions of *The Christian Faith*, is a process of refinement as Schleiermacher struggles to clarify in his own mind the true essence of religion. He knows that piety is at the heart of religion, but how is that to be set forth in contrast to the knowing and doing, the metaphysics and the ethics, that the intellectual world of his day takes for religion? Piety, he declares, is about being in relation to God. All that religion entails derives from this relation. Hence it is possible to determine in outline, through the lens of his concept of piety, Schleiermacher's philosophy of God, his anthropology, and also his christology.

Schleiermacher describes piety as the awareness of one's absolute dependence for one's very existence upon another, an awareness that takes place in self-consciousness. This for Schleiermacher is the essence of religion. "God," in Schleiermacher's view, is the "whence" of one's existence, experienced in this awareness of one's absolute dependence. "As regards the identification of absolute dependence with 'relation to God'... this is to be understood in the sense that the *Whence* of our receptive and active existence, as implied in this self-consciousness, is to be designated by the word 'God', and that this is for us the really original signification of that word."[14] Schleiermacher, therefore, identifies God as that on which existence itself depends. His understanding of God has for its context those ultimate questions which are necessary for a proper understanding of the relationship between God and the world. Here, we have Schleiermacher's basic philosophical position regarding the notion of God.

In Schleiermacher's basic anthropology, the human being is that which is conscious of itself as absolutely dependent upon another for its whole existence. Piety is experiencing this self-consciousness as a tendency toward that other, that upon which one is utterly dependent. Piety is submitting onself to the impulse toward God. "Religious experience... consists precisely in this, that we are aware of this tendency to God-consciousness as a living impulse; but such an impulse can only proceed from the true inner nature of the being which it goes to constitute."[15]

The impulse toward God is what constitutes the human being in the depths of its nature. The human being is essentially spirit, mediating its experiences through the body. "If we now take man first of all purely on his inner side, as a self-active being in whom God-consciousness is possible—that is, as spirit; then, from this point of view, his bodily side, which is not the man himself, belongs originally to this material world into which the spirit enters. Only gradually does it become for the spirit the instrument and means of expression... but first of all and primarily it mediates the stimulating influences of the world upon the spirit."[16] As the body mediates the created world it becomes the means through which the spirit both experiences existence and expresses its experiences. However, the God-consciousness toward which the spirit tends, the God-consciousness which is possible for the spirit, has been obscured by sin. And so for the impulse toward God to be satisfied, a redemption is necessary.

Schleiermacher distinguishes between the feeling of absolute dependence and the God-consciousness achieved through redemption. The one is an impulse toward God; the other, the satisfaction of that impulse. Interestingly, in *The Christian Faith* he also makes a distinction between the inner impulse to God-consciousness and the faculty for attaining such consciousness. "The predisposition to God-consciousness, as an inner impulse, includes the consciousness of a faculty of attaining, by means of the human organism, to those states of self-consciousness in which the God-consciousness can realize itself."[17] The human organism here refers to the body. Schleiermacher then comments that "the tendency toward God-consciousness would be altogether nugatory if the condition necessary for it in human life could not be evoked."[18] The impulse toward God would be more or less worthless were there not, in the human being itself, the mechanism for the impulse to be satisfied. In Schleiermacher's view, without "redemption" there would be only the impulse toward God, and not the possibility of that impulse being satisfied.

Schleiermacher defines redemption as follows:

> Redemption [*Erlösung*] . . . signifies in general a passage from an evil condition, which is represented as a state of captivity or constraint, into a better condition . . . the evil condition can only consist in an obstruction or arrest of the vitality of the higher self-consciousness. . . . We may give to this condition, in its most extreme form, the name of *Godlessness,* or, better, *God-forgetfulness.* But we must not think this means a state in which it is quite impossible for the God-consciousness to be kindled. For if that were so, then, in the first place, the lack of a thing which lay outside of one's nature could not be felt to be an evil condition; and in the second place, a re-creating in the strict sense would then be needed in order to make good this lack, and that is not included in the idea of redemption. The possibility, then, of rekindling the God-consciousness remains in reserve even where the evil condition of that consciousness is painted in the darkest colors. . . . [N]o satisfaction of the impulse towards the God-consciousness will be possible . . . if such a satisfaction is to be attained, a redemption is necessary.[19]

God-consciousness has been obscured. It must be redeemed, recovered, but it does not have to be created anew. The possibility for God-consciousness remains no matter how badly human nature has been corrupted by sin. And this possibility is never absent, although a redemption is necessary to realize it. This brings us to Schleiermacher's christology: Christ is the Redeemer.

Schleiermacher's theology is thoroughly Christocentric. Christianity, he says, "is essentially distinguished from other . . . faiths by the fact that in it everything is related to the redemption accomplished by Jesus of Nazareth."[20] And for Schleiermacher, Christ is more than merely an exemplar. The role of Redeemer is unique to him, and his redeeming power is effective for all.

> Accordingly, in Christianity the relation of the founder to the members of the communion is quite different from what it is in the other religions. For those other founders are represented as having been, as it were, arbitrarily elevated from the mass of similar or not very different men, and as receiving just as much for themselves as for other people whatever they do receive in the way of divine doctrine and precept. Thus even an adherent of those faiths will hardly deny that God could just as well have given the law through another as through Moses, and the revelation could just as well have been given through another as through Mohammed. But Christ is distinguished from all others as Redeemer alone and for all, and is in no wise regarded as having been at any time in need of redemption himself; and is therefore separated from the beginning from all other men, and endowed with redeeming power from his birth.[21]

Redemption (*Erlösung*), Schleiermacher observes, is posited by the Christian "as a thing which has been universally and completely accomplished by Jesus of Nazareth."[22] But how does that redemption take place? In the historical Jesus of Nazareth a perfect God-consciousness existed, which enabled all other human beings to achieve that same God-consciousness. Thus it is Jesus' piety, his perfect God-consciousness, his relation to God, that constitutes his unique redeeming quality. Schleiermacher remarks that "to ascribe to Christ an absolutely powerful God-consciousness, and to attribute to Him an existence of God in Him, are exactly the same thing."[23] With this remark Schleiermacher's definition of piety expands further. It follows that the God-consciousness toward which the human spirit tends is a matter of having within one the life of God.

What Schleiermacher understands by the God-consciousness that is accomplished for all human beings involves the human being sharing the life of God as a consequence of salvation through Jesus Christ.

Schleiermacher envisages a philosophical situation in which the human being *as human being* is conscious of itself as absolutely dependent upon an "other" for existence itself. In this situation the human being is characterized by an impulse toward—a reaching out for—that other. But the God-consciousness toward which the human spirit tends has been lost through sin. Jesus is the Redeemer, who needs no redemption himself but who, through his own perfect God-consciousness, is able to remove the obstacle to God-consciousness for the rest of humanity. However, the consciousness of absolute dependence, the impulse toward the other on which human existence utterly depends, would obtain independently of Jesus' life or act of redemption.

The Mediation of Knowledge

One of the main contentions of this work is that Schleiermacher has something special to offer a defense of Christian faith—something that can meet the two central epistemological challenges. This section discusses Schleiermacher's views with respect to the role of the created world in the mediation of knowledge, even the knowledge of God that comes through revelation. A future section will focus on the question of evidence.

Schleiermacher is much criticized for failing to give an adequate account of the mediation of knowledge. Thiemann's criticism, described in chapter 3, is typical. He maintains that Schleiermacher, in his presentation of self-consciousness, adopts what Thiemann terms an epistemological foundationalism. Thiemann's condemnation of Schleiermacher's religious epistemology centers on the role that Schleiermacher accords to "intuition." Intuition is one of the components of piety in Schleiermacher's thought, and Thiemann takes Schleiermacher's description of "piety-as-such" to be an appeal to an intuitive knowing, an experience of God that is prior to any particular historical or cultural involvement. As already noted in chapter 3, Thiemann says that for Schleiermacher, "[r]evelation is a self-conscious experience, but it does not directly engage our knowing and doing";[24] and, referring to Schleiermacher's "experience of absolute dependence," this "removes one from the world of particular times and places, of distinct subjects and objects, and allows an immediate relation to God through the transparent tissue of feeling."[25]

In spite of the remarks in the previous section on the mediating role of the body in Schleiermacher's anthropology, some material in his writings does suggest that he makes no allowance for the mediation of knowledge in matters of faith. It is possible to discern two reasons for this. In the first place, Schleiermacher is determined at all times to offer an alternative to the brand of speculative thinking that results in either the version of metaphysics or the version of ethics that he opposes. In the second place, he is, as he writes, in the process of working out what that alternative should be; as a result, some of what he says will be open to criticism and some of what he says will be subject to his own revisions or subsequent clarifications. These two factors must be borne in mind when reading Schleiermacher. Take, for example, the following passage: "Religion's essence is neither thinking nor acting, but intuition and feeling. It wishes to intuit the universe, wishes devoutly to overhear the universe's own manifestations and actions, longs to be grasped and filled by the universe's immediate influences in childlike passivity."[26] Schleiermacher is struggling here to differentiate piety from speculative theology and ethics, and at the same time he is fumbling for a more precise account of what constitutes piety. It is precisely this sort of passage that brings up the questionable notion of intuitive unmediated knowledge of God and leaves Schleiermacher vulnerable to criticism such as Thiemann's.

In light of Schleiermacher's identification of knowing and doing with speculative metaphysics and ethical systems, one must ask whether his antipathy toward knowing and doing means, as Thiemann thinks it does, that he regards the feeling of absolute dependence on God as unmediated by time and place. This inference needs closer examination.

In *Speeches*, the faculty of intuition is of great significance, as is that of feeling. In the second speech, Schleiermacher explores the intimate connection between these two faculties as he begins to work out the essence of religion. He will develop this line of thought when he attempts to clarify the essence of piety in the first and second editions of *The Christian Faith*. At the early stage of *Speeches*, he states that the essence of religion is "neither thinking nor acting, but intuition and feeling."[27] It should be noted, however, that he continues, "religion maintains its own sphere and its own character only by completely removing itself from the sphere and character of speculation as well as from that of praxis."[28]

"Speculation" here refers not to "knowing" but to philosophical constructions that condone skepticism in religious matters.[29] "Praxis" here refers not to "doing" but to a codification of ethics based on a false understanding of morality. Praxis "is an art [which arrives] at an impoverished uniformity that knows only a single ideal and lays this as the basis everywhere."[30] In an allusion to Kant's *Critique of Practical Reason*, Schleiermacher remarks of the "morality" to which he objects that it "proceeds from the consciousness of freedom; it wishes to extend freedom's realm to infinity and to make everything subservient to it."[31]

Schleiermacher, therefore, does not intend to distance religion from the connection with knowing and doing that belongs to the cognitive state, but rather intends to distance it from a speculative theology that condones religious skepticism, and from a system of ethics that treats the human being as the source of morality. Religion, for Schleiermacher, is quite different from these last two disciplines. His model of religious truth is emphatically not that of deductions from a basic intuition, conceived as a foundational justification for belief. In his *Speeches*, Schleiermacher is struggling to say what the essence of religion in fact is; later, he will talk of it as being in relation with God. From the very beginning, however, he is quite clear about what it is not. It is not speculative theology, and it is not ethics, but something quite different. Schleiermacher wants to say that it is not a human construction.

In describing intuition, Schleiermacher compares it to religion. Both, he says, are self-contained, do not depend on other perceptions, and are not derived from their connection to anything else. In matters of religion, it is not a question of certain basic truths on the basis of which religion is constructed, because religion is not a human construction. In this respect, religion is true "in itself." Schleiermacher comments that religion "knows nothing about derivation and connection, for among all things religion can encounter, that is what its nature most opposes. Not only an individual fact [*Tatsache*] or deed [*Handlung*] that one could call original [*ursprünglich*] or first [*erst*] but everything in religion is immediate and true for itself."³²

Richard Crouter, the editor and translator of the 1988 edition of *Speeches*, draws attention to the fact that *Tatsache, Handlung, erst,* and *ursprünglich* are used by Fichte to express the first principle of consciousness, the principle of identity, or A = A. Thus, observes Crouter, there is no doubt that Schleiermacher's target here is Fichte's *Science of Knowledge*.³³ Schleiermacher is rejecting Fichte's view that religion is a system which derives from first principles. Immediately following the passage on religion quoted above, Schleiermacher urges his readers to engage in "sensible intuition" (*sinnliche Anschauung*):

> A system of intuitions? [*Ein System von Anschauungen . . . ?*] Can you imagine anything stranger? Do views, and especially views of the infinite, allow themselves to be brought into a system? . . . I speak your language in these matters, for it would be an infinite business, and you are not accustomed to connect the concept of something infinite with the term "system," but rather the concept of something that is limited and completed in its limitation. Elevate yourselves at once . . . to that infinite dimension of sensible intuition, to the wondrous and celebrated starry sky. [*Erhebt Euch einmal . . . zu jenem Unendlichen der sinnlichen Anschauung, dem bewunderten und gefeierten Sternenhimmel.*] The astronomical theories, which orient a thousand suns with their world systems around a common point and seek for each common point again a higher world system that could be its centre, and so on into infinity, outwardly and inwardly—surely you would not want to call this a system of intuitions as such?³⁴

The point Schleiermacher makes is that intuition, which is something like the essence of religion, is not amenable to systematization. He is working out his idea of the essence of piety—a "being-in-relationship-to-God" that cannot be brought within a system constructed by philosophical speculation. Crouter points out that the expression *sinnliche Anschauung* is traceable to Kant's *Critique of Pure Reason,* and comments on the similarity between the second half of the passage quoted above and Kant's tribute to the wondrous effect on the human mind of the "starry heavens above me and the moral law within me," at the end of the *Critique of Practical Reason*.[35] Crouter also remarks that "Schleiermacher uses the term for our immediate apprehension of objects in the world in which concepts play no mediating role." Yet the term *sinnliche Anschauung* normally refers to a perception by the senses, implying the mediation of the finite, and Schleiermacher specifically seems to envisage a mediating role for the *concept* of the "starry sky."

The latter interpretation is supported by Schleiermacher's dictum, "Intuition without feeling is nothing and can have neither the proper origin nor the proper force; feeling without intuition is also nothing." Crouter observes that in making this statement, Schleiermacher plays on the Kantian dictum, "Thoughts without content are empty, intuitions without concepts are blind."[36] This allusion adds strength to the view that the *sensible* intuition envisaged by Schleiermacher is unavoidably bound up with the experiences of the senses. Thus, it would seem to go some way toward countering Thiemann's criticism that piety-as-such refers to an intuitive, unmediated knowledge of God. But in order to explore this criticism further, particularly Thiemann's contention that Schleiermacher's "experience of absolute dependence" removes one from the world of particular times and places, it is necessary to look closely at what Schleiermacher understands by "feeling" (*Gefühl*).

The Feeling of Absolute Dependence

Feeling is the component that combines with intuition to constitute the essence of true religion in *Speeches,* and when Schleiermacher pursues his exploration of piety in the two editions of *The Christian Faith,* he places the stress on feeling. Schleiermacher describes piety as the *feeling* of absolute dependence. In light of this stress on *Gefühl*, Schleiermacher is widely accused of subjectivism. Subjectivism in this context would consist of producing from one's own mental resources that which one calls "God."

Schleiermacher's fiercest and most notable critic was Hegel, his colleague and rival on the theological faculty at Berlin. Hegel's lectures on philosophy of religion brought into the open his clash with Schleiermacher. Each sought to determine the principles that would ground the theology of the Evangelical Church of the Prussian Union.[37] Hegel's dispute with Schleiermacher reached its climax with Hegel's foreword to H. F. W. Hinrichs's *Die Religion im inneren Verhältnisse zur Wissenschaft* of 1822[38] (about the same time as the publication of the first edition of Schleiermacher's *The Christian Faith*) and Hegel's second series of lectures in 1824. There is no evidence, however, that during these years Hegel was familiar with Schleiermacher's actual text in *The Christian Faith*.[39]

In the following extract from his 1824 lectures, Hegel criticizes the subjectivism of those who put the notion of feeling at the center of religion. In addition to Schleiermacher's notion of piety, Hegel probably had in mind the theology of F. H. Jacobi, who, following David Hume, established a close connection between faith and feeling:

> Because knowledge of God does not fall within the comprehension of reason, there coheres with this standpoint the view that consciousness of God is rather sought only in the form of *feeling*—that religion has feeling as its source, and that the relationship of the human spirit to God is to be confined only to the sphere of feeling and is not to be transposed into thought or into comprehension. Surely if God and divine things are excluded from the realm of necessary and substantial subjectivity, if knowledge is excluded from this realm, then nothing remains but the realm of contingent subjectivity; that is the realm of feeling. If in regard to God we could appeal only to feeling, then we would have to wonder how any kind of objectivity is still attributed to this content, i.e., to God.[40]

Among modern critics, Michael Buckley also condemns Schleiermacher's theology on the ground that it is subjectivist. As Buckley interprets Schleiermacher, "God is given to human beings, not fundamentally through the universe, but through and with self-consciousness. . . . The evidence for God is no longer nature. It is to be human nature. The human is the basis for the affirmation of the divine. . . . This revolution in theological foundations elicited and fashioned its own correlative atheism. . . . God was not part of human appropriation but of human projection."[41]

With Schleiermacher in mind, Buckley argues that such appeals to human nature, in order to defend theological assertions, generated Feuerbach's demand that human nature be recognized as infinite.[42] Here, Buckley's interpretation seems to coincide with the widely held view that Feuerbach's thought represents the logical working out of the meaning and implications of Schleiermacher's thought—an interpretation that should not go unchallenged.[43] The attitude of Feuerbach toward Schleiermacher was colored by Feuerbach's own quarrel with Hegel. Smarting from Hegel's criticisms, Feuerbach commented in his lectures, "The so-called speculative philosophers have ridiculed me for putting down the feeling of dependency as the source of religion. They have held the words 'feeling of dependency' in low esteem ever since Hegel, in response to Schleiermacher—who, as we know, found the essence of religion in man's feeling of dependency—remarked that then a dog must also have religion because he feels dependent on his master."[44]

Feuerbach here claims support from Schleiermacher for his own view that religion is a human projection. Yet, as the following quotation makes clear, Feuerbach was aware of the gulf between his own approach and that of Schleiermacher: "I do not reproach Schleiermacher as Hegel does, because he makes religion a matter of feeling, but only because he did not and could not, given his confinement within theology, come to draw the conclusions that necessarily follow from his position. I reproach him because he did not have the courage to see and to acknowledge that objectively God himself is nothing other than the essence of feeling, if subjectively feeling is the main thing in religion."[45] Unlike Hegel, Feuerbach blames Schleiermacher not for having reduced religion to a question of sentiment, but for failing to follow through to its necessary consequences the fact, as Feuerbach sees it, that religion is a matter of sentiment.

There is no denying that Schleiermacher's writings sometimes give occasion for the charge of subjectivism. As Schleiermacher develops his thinking, however, he takes account of the criticisms that are brought against him and clarifies his terminology. As we have seen, Schleiermacher is already quite clear in *Speeches* about what piety is *not*. His positive teaching on the essence of true religion, culminating in his account of piety as the feeling of absolute dependence, *das schlechthinnig Abhängigkeitsgefühl*, develops over a period of time. In *Speeches* he talks of piety in terms of "worship [of] the deity in holy silence," contemplation of "the eternal and holy being," and "feelings for and with" the eternal and holy being.[46] He introduces the notion of the feeling of absolute dependence in the lengthy title of paragraph 9 of the first edition of *The Christian Faith*, in which he states the essence of piety:

> The common element in all pious emotions, thus the essence of piety, is this: that we are conscious of ourselves as absolutely dependent, that is, that we feel dependent on God [*dass wir uns unsrer selbst als schlechthin abhängig bewusst sind, dass heisst, dass wir uns abhängig fühlen von Gott*].[47]

This early description of piety is, admittedly, unsatisfactory. It seems to reduce God to one element in the world, or to present God as merely a projection that derives from some sort of Romantic notion of feeling. It lays Schleiermacher open to precisely the criticism that Buckley makes with regard to subjectivity. It can even suggest a pantheistic understanding of God.[48] In restating the consciousness of self as absolutely dependent in terms of feeling dependent on God, Schleiermacher does not adequately distinguish the way in which human beings are dependent on God from the way in which they are dependent on the created world. In the words of Julia Lamm, "the key term *schlechthin abhängig* seems to be compromised by the last clause of the proposition."[49] As Lamm points out, "absolutely dependent" is compromised when it is re-expressed to include the explicit reference to God, but without the word "absolutely" (*schlechthin*) to qualify the word "dependent" (*abhängig*). Schleiermacher himself recognized the inadequacies of the statement in the first edition of *The Christian Faith*, and revised it in the title of paragraph 4 of the second edition:

> The common element in all howsoever diverse expressions of piety, by which these are cojointly distinguished from all other feelings, or, in other words, the self-identical essence of piety, is this: the consciousness of being absolutely dependent [*dass wir uns unsrer selbst als schlechthin abhängig*], or, which is the same thing, of being in relation with God.[50]

This revision is significant. The consciousness of absolute dependence is equated not with a *feeling* of dependence on God, but with a *consciousness of being in a relationship* with God—a relationship that involves absolute dependence upon God. Later in paragraph 4 Schleiermacher uses the term "the feeling of absolute dependence," *das schlechthinnig Abhängigkeitsgefühl,* to denote piety. The essence of religion is therefore the consciousness of oneself as being in a relationship of absolute dependence upon God as the source of one's existence.

There is other important evidence in the second edition of *The Christian Faith* supporting the argument that Schleiermacher does *not* understand the experience of God to be somehow disembodied and ahistorical; that he does not consider that it "removes one from the world of particular times and places, of distinct subjects and objects."[51] Rather, in this edition he sees the experience of God as mediated in the historical living out of one's life. In discussing the feeling of absolute dependence, Schleiermacher does not talk about isolated experience as such. On the contrary, this feeling of absolute dependence "cannot exist in a single moment as such, because such a moment is always determined, as regards its total content, by what is *given,* and thus by objects towards which we have a feeling of freedom."[52]

Furthermore, according to Schleiermacher, people are unable to feel themselves absolutely dependent upon the whence of their existence, without at the same time being conscious of their limited dependency upon the world. Human beings, he claims, have a limited feeling of freedom in relation to the world and are able to exercise a certain amount of influence upon it. Their dependence on the world is therefore not absolute. Schleiermacher concludes that self-consciousness of this limited dependence always accompanies the self-consciousness of absolute dependence.

Thiemann's criticism of Schleiermacher is answered at this point. In holding that without the consciousness of limited dependence there is no consciousness of absolute dependence, Schleiermacher clearly holds that the experience of God never occurs outside the experience of the world. Self-consciousness of this limited dependence upon the world, he argues, is in fact necessary for the self-consciousness of absolute dependence, since it is precisely the consciousness that *any* free activity in relation to the world derives from a source outside the human being that constitutes the feeling of absolute dependence. In Schleiermacher's words,

> [T]he self-consciousness which accompanies all our activity, and therefore, since that is never zero, accompanies our whole existence, and negatives absolute freedom, is itself precisely a consciousness of absolute dependence; for it is the consciousness that the whole of our spontaneous activity comes from a source outside of us in just the same sense in which anything towards which we should have a feeling of absolute freedom must have proceeded entirely from ourselves. But without any feeling of freedom a feeling of absolute dependence would not be possible.[53]

In short, the feeling of absolute dependence is never found in, as it were, pure form. Though it constitutes the "highest grade of human self-consciousness," it is never found isolated from a consciousness of the world, since "in its actual occurrence it is never separated from the lower."[54]

God as a Permanent Accompaniment to All Human Experience

In teasing out from Schleiermacher's account of piety his view of how the experience of God is mediated in the historical living out of one's life, one particular feature of his religious epistemology has emerged that will prove crucial: for Schleiermacher, God is a permanent accompaniment to all human experience. We have seen that for Schleiermacher, the experience of God takes place in the experience of absolute dependence. This experience, says Schleiermacher, is given in the very self-consciousness that "accompanies our whole existence."[55] Schleiermacher's depiction of the feeling of absolute dependence describes, in a Kantian way, not an isolated experience but rather a state which characterizes all human experience. Lamm observes that for Schleiermacher, "this feeling of absolute dependence is part of the necessary and universal structures of human existence, of the human constitution; it is an 'inward permanent datum' that makes God-consciousness possible."[56] Schleiermacher thus understands this consciousness of oneself as absolutely dependent as something that is always "there" as the background to any experience that counts as human experience. It is through this background self-consciousness that God's revelation takes place. Schleiermacher says that "if we speak of an original revelation of God to man or in man, the meaning will always be just this, that, along with the absolute dependence which characterizes not only man but all temporal existence, there is given to man also the immediate self-consciousness of it, which becomes a consciousness of God. In whatever measure this actually takes place during the course of a personality through time, in just that measure do we ascribe piety to the individual."[57] Schleiermacher, clearly, acknowledges that the experience of absolute dependence will be more explicit on certain occasions and less explicit on others, yet his position is that the experience of God is not confined to particular experiences. The consciousness of God characterizes *all* temporal existence of the human person.

Evidence for the Existence of God

In discussing the classical arguments for the existence of God in *The Christian Faith,* Schleiermacher's language indicates that he thinks the proofs are superseded. His lengthy title to paragraph 33 (§33) reads: "This feeling of absolute dependence, in which our self-consciousness in general represents the finitude of our being (cf. §8, 2), is therefore not an accidental element, or a thing which varies from person to person, but is a universal element of life; and the recognition of this fact entirely takes the place, for the system of doctrine, of all the so-called proofs of the existence of God."[58] Schleiermacher does not maintain that the classical arguments are irrelevant to faith, or that there is no necessity to ground in some way the existence of God. Rather, the notion that God is present in human conscious activity as such precludes the necessity of employing the classical arguments, on the grounds that the existence of God is self-evident.

Schleiermacher makes a second point. The arguments for the existence of God have been superseded by the feeling of absolute dependence, which is universal, common to all. The feeling of absolute dependence "and the

God-consciousness contained in it are a fundamental moment of human life." And "even supposing its universality could be disputed, still no obligation would arise for the system of doctrine to prove the existence of God; that would be an entirely superfluous task since proofs could only produce an objective consciousness which would not in any way generate piety."[59]

According to Schleiermacher, therefore, it is self-evident in the light of human experience that God exists as the whence of human existence. In this sense there is evidence to support the view that God exists. To say that God exists is not an irrational assertion. It can be spoken of in rational terms, and to the extent that any elaboration of the assertion accords with human experience, it can be grounded or justified in human experience. However if this were not the case, if the existence of God were not self-evident in the feeling of absolute dependence, then it would be pointless to attempt to prove the existence of God. No awareness of God that was "outside" this consciousness of the self as absolutely dependent upon another would be of any use. It could not generate piety. In other words, it could not generate faith.

Both Thiemann and Buckley believe that Schleiermacher attempts to prove the prevenience (Thiemann) or the existence (Buckley) of God through the provision of evidence. In Buckley's view, as noted earlier, Schleiermacher takes human nature as evidence for the existence of God. It is possible to affirm the divine because of a sure knowledge of the human. According to Thiemann, "Schleiermacher's defense of revelation rests upon his famous argument for absolute dependence in paragraph 4 of *The Christian Faith.*"[60] Thiemann's concern is to defend the doctrine of revelation, and he attributes the same concern to Schleiermacher. These claims of Buckley and Thiemann must be investigated to see whether they are correct. And if they are not correct, then what is Schleiermacher's aim? And what is his attitude toward what might be thought of as evidence for religious belief?

Buckley, I argue, simply misconstrues Schleiermacher's intention, which is not at all to prove the existence of God. Schleiermacher merely thinks that there is an inevitability about positing the existence of God, once we have agreed on the concept to which the word "God" is being applied. The inevitability of positing God's existence is illustrated with reference to Schleiermacher's central notion of the feeling of absolute dependence, *das schlechthinnig Abhängigkeitsgefühl,* which for him sums up the essence of true religion or piety. As we have seen, by the time Schleiermacher uses this term it is equated with a consciousness of being in a relationship with God—a relationship that involves absolute dependence upon God.[61] The essence of religion is the consciousness of oneself as being in relationship of absolute dependence upon God as the source of one's existence. According to Schleiermacher's mature position, then, there is an undeniable inevitability about positing the existence of God. This will always be the case when human experience is interpreted in a metaphysical context, and despite his criticisms of a Fichtean-type metaphysics, Schleiermacher does interpret the human being in a metaphysical context. "That God exists" is not the primary message of this type of theology; rather, "this is how the relationship works between God [the Whence of human existence] and the human being." Outside the relationship between God and the human being this type of theology has nothing to say, since for Schleiermacher there is no "outside" this relationship.

Thiemann thinks that Schleiermacher is trying to justify the doctrine of revelation, but Schleiermacher's Protestantism does not require that sort of justification. Paragraph 4 is not a defense of revelation but an imaginative interpretation of the classic understanding of the revelatory event, which itself needs no defense. On the classic understanding, when God chooses to reveal God's self to the human being, the human being is given the grace to respond in faith. (There is always the acknowledgement, explicit or implicit, that this situation pertains because of the cross of Christ.) Faith is recognizing and accepting the relationship between the human being and God, which is the relationship between sinful subject and gracious sovereign. In Schleiermacher's view, revelation means that for the human being there is the consciousness of the relationship of absolute dependence upon another—a consciousness which (through redemption in Christ) becomes a consciousness of God. Faith is to live in the light of this relationship. This is the essence of the Christian religion, the measure of piety. Schleiermacher is describing, not defending, revelation; he is reflecting on the classical Protestant teaching that what is revealed in revelation is the true situation of the human being in relation to God.

Another aspect of Schleiermacher's theology is too important to pass over without mention here: Schleiermacher believes in the universality of grace. Schleiermacher talks of an "original" revelation, and here he refers to a revelation that is prior to and inclusive of specific revelatory experiences. This description of revelation does indeed apply to the way in which revelation occurs, when God so chooses, as the Word is proclaimed and accepted in faith in the Evangelical Church of the Prussian Union. In paragraph 4, however, Schleiermacher also talks of the revelation that occurs in the life of each human being in the actual living out of daily life.

Schleiermacher believes that "through the power of redemption there will one day be a universal restoration of all souls."[62] If we are redeemed through Christ, then death has been conquered. Schleiermacher cites 1 Cor. 15.26 ("The last enemy to be destroyed is death") and 1 Cor. 15.55 ("O Death, where is thy victory? O Death, where is thy sting?").[63] When he states that there can be no permanently binding doctrinal formulas, his underlying intention is to convey that there can be no formulas *that one has to believe on pain of eternal damnation*. The qualification is important. Schleiermacher in fact rejects the very notion of eternal damnation itself. Thus grace is universal.

Returning to the question of evidence, Schleiermacher does not set out to prove that God exists or to defend the doctrine of revelation. In *Speeches* he intends to prove that piety, not speculative philosophy, is the essence of religion. *The Christian Faith* is a dogmatic work, in which he states quite clearly,

> Dogmatics must . . . presuppose intuitive certainty of faith; and thus, as far as the God-consciousness in general is concerned, what it has to do is not to effect its recognition but to explicate its content. That such proofs [to prove the existence of God] are not the concern of Dogmatics is obvious also from the fact that it is impossible to give them dogmatic form; for we cannot go back to Scripture and symbolical books, since they themselves do not prove, but simply assert. Moreover, he for whom such assertion is authoritative needs no further proof.[64]

The relationship between God and the human being that Schleiermacher ponders is revealed in Scripture and requires no further justification for one who has faith. There would be no point in proving this relationship to one who did not have faith, since objective knowledge of God, if it were possible, would not bring about faith. Yet that is not to say that Schleiermacher's reflections are not in some way grounded in human experience; it is not to say that the image that he paints to explain what the Protestant Church understands by revelation is not illustrated in terms of a specific anthropology. And to the extent that Schleiermacher's reflection on the God-world relationship accords with human experience, he necessarily provides some sort of grounding, some sort of evidence, hence some sort of justification for the existence of God. Likewise, to the extent that his illustration of the revelatory event accords with human experience, he is necessarily concerned, at some level, with proof. It is proof at the level of asserting that to believe in this way is not irrational; that to believe in this way makes sense in terms of the phenomena that are encountered in the ordinary living out of human life. Furthermore, in reflecting on the God-world relationship Schleiermacher necessarily provides an anthropology and a philosophical understanding of God. Thus his philosophical theology shares with the classical proofs a sense that the existence of God needs in some way to be grounded. He is in fact refining rather than repudiating the proofs.

There is a sense in which the notion of God *does* explain for Schleiermacher the feeling of absolute dependence. Although he does not explicitly put forward deductive a posteriori arguments for God's existence, it could nonetheless be argued that such arguments are implicit in his work. He does, after all, say certain things about God on the basis of the empirical fact that human beings feel themselves to be absolutely dependent on the whence of their existence. In his scheme, the existence of God does explain the feeling of absolute dependence. With reference to the traditional arguments, it has been shown that deductive a posteriori arguments for the existence of God retain their limited usefulness insofar as they name conditions which any valid, fuller explanation must satisfy, but that any attempt at a substantive explanation of God would contradict the notion of God's transcendence. Insofar as there is an implicit argument for God's existence to be deduced from the feeling of absolute dependence as put forward by Schleiermacher, does what he has to say about God merely name conditions which must be satisfied if more is to be said, or does he arrive at a substantive presentation of God?

Typical of the way in which Schleiermacher shapes his doctrine of God is the following passage from *The Christian Faith*. He has just stated that the meaning of revelation is that the consciousness of oneself as absolutely dependent becomes a consciousness of God. He sees this God-consciousness as a background consciousness, always present in human conscious activity. He says nothing about the "content" of God, but merely that God—whatever that might be—is in some sense given to the human being in piety. He then sets out certain conditions regarding what *may not* be said of God:

> On the other hand, any possibility of God being in any way *given* is entirely excluded, because anything that is outwardly given must be given as an object exposed to our counter-influence, however slight this may be. The transference of the idea of God to any perceptible object, unless one is all the time conscious that it is a piece of purely arbitrary symbolism, is always a corruption, whether it be a temporary transference, i.e. a theophany, or a constitutive transference, in which God is represented as permanently in a particular perceptible existence.[65]

God is not "outwardly" (*äusserlich*) given, as a created object would be—in a way that would render what is given vulnerable to human influence. Also, while a created object may symbolize God's presence, God is not and cannot be a material object.

These two conditions follow four others that have already been set forth, though without being named as "conditions." First, the word "God" cannot be used outside the subject's relation to the whence of its existence. Second, the only content of the idea of God is as the whence of human existence known in human self-consciousness. Third, God is only known in relationship. And fourth, any further content of the idea of "God" cannot be found outside this relationship. Two more conditions may be added to the list based on our further exploration of Schleiermacher. That is, we may not talk about God as though God were not distinct from the world. And finally, we may not talk about God as though God were "outside" the world. These conditions summarize all that Schleiermacher says about God. Rather than offering a substantive explanation of God, he offers a series of conditions which must be satisfied if more is to be said.

Nicholas Lash in his work *Easter in Ordinary* arrives at a similar conclusion regarding Schleiermacher's use of the term "God." Schleiermacher is simply stating that this should be the way in which Christians use the word "God": they use it to designate the "whence" of the feeling of absolute dependence. "The remark, therefore, is what Wittgenstein would have called a 'grammatical' remark; it does *not* constitute an *empirical* claim of any kind. To put it another way . . . Schleiermacher is indicating one of the *rules* according to which the word 'God,' which we have inherited, is appropriately to be used."[66]

For Lash, Schleiermacher is safeguarding the concept of God as it has been traditionally understood and handed down. Thus, according to Lash, Schleiermacher is justified in identifying the non-objectifiable "whence" of the feeling of absolute dependence with God, because he (Schleiermacher) considers that this is the way in which Christians have used and should use the word "God."

It is worth noting that Lash's rule is a negative rather than a positive one. God is the "whence" that cannot be objectified. The basis of the rule is the fact that God cannot be viewed as a finite object. Similarly, all the conditions that have been drawn from Schleiermacher's thought are negative rules. There is even an implicit negative, for example, in the condition that "God" is distinct from the world. How the distinction is to be drawn is left open. The force of the rule lies in the fact that God is not to be understood as merely identical with the world.

Besides supplying these negative conditions for valid discourse about God, however, Schleiermacher does implicitly include a positive, substantive claim. The whence of human existence which human beings name "God" must exist for human beings to feel themselves absolutely dependent upon it. One cannot interpret Schleiermacher as saying that the whence of human existence may or may not exist. Furthermore, the whence is the necessary ground for self-consciousness, and as such it is that which grounds the cognitive status of sentences about God. Thus it is not possible to have knowledge without the reality of "God."

As we have seen, Schleiermacher explicitly dismisses the traditional arguments for the existence of God as irrelevant to piety. Yet to the extent that he takes the existence of "God" as the explanation for the feeling of absolute dependence—and the traditional arguments are, therefore, implicit in his work—he not only sets out a series of conditions which must be satisfied when God is explained, but his account of God-consciousness fulfills one of their chief functions: that of grounding the cognitive status of sentences about God.

When we turn to Rahner, whose attitude toward the classical proofs is arguably similar to Schleiermacher's, it will be necessary to discuss how appropriate is this type of "evidence" for the existence of God, and to revisit the claim that evidence of this sort represents an unacceptable foundationalism.

CHAPTER 5

Rahner's "God"

In portraying the consciousness of God as the permanent background to human conscious experience, Schleiermacher has provided a way of thinking about knowledge of God without compromising the notion that knowledge of God is radically distinct from knowledge of finite objects. It recognizes the infinite difference between the transcendent and the transcended, and yet allows for the claim that knowledge of God is mediated by the finite. The aim in this chapter is to set forth Karl Rahner's religious epistemology and the surprising similarities between his and Schleiermacher's thinking on the same issues.

From Rahner's extensive collection of published works it will suffice to draw on three. The first is *Geist in Welt* (*Spirit in the World*),[1] in which Rahner attempts to work out how metaphysical knowledge can be possible given that there is no knowledge unmediated by the material world. Focusing solely on article 7, question 84 of the *Summa Theologiae* of Thomas Aquinas, *Spirit in the World* is an examination and interpretation of Thomas's view that human knowing can reach beyond the reality accessible to immediate human experience (the world) and know the metaphysical. This transcendental reaching beyond the finite world is, for Rahner, the fundamental characteristic of the human being. Rahner develops this notion in his other early philosophical work, *Hörer des Wortes*

(*Hearer of the Word*),² in which he describes the *human* being as the being who, in history, listens for a possible revelation of God. It is here that Rahner first sets out his argument that God, as the infinite horizon of human transcendence, necessarily exists. The third work from which this chapter draws is Rahner's much later systematic study, *Grundkurs des Glaubens (Foundations of Christian Faith)*.³

The presumption here is that there is no disjunction between the earlier two works and *Foundations of Christian Faith*. Some commentators have argued that Rahner's later theology can be read as logically independent of his philosophy.⁴ This chapter adopts the more conventional interpretation that Rahner's theology at all times remains linked to a philosophical vision, the essentials of which are set out in his earlier works. Neither *Spirit in the World* nor *Hearer of the Word* can be regarded as purely philosophical in nature. In these works, as in *Foundations*, Rahner's philosophy of God and his philosophical anthropology are intimately bound up with his theology. Throughout all three works, there are no substantial differences in the way his philosophical understanding is combined with his understanding of revelation, particularly the mystery of grace.

Transcendental Thomism

Transcendental Thomism, which originated with Joseph Maréchal, attempts to apply insights regarding transcendence learned from Kant to the theology of Thomas Aquinas. Transcendental knowledge, according to Kant, is knowledge not of objects but of the necessary a priori conditions of our cognition of objects; the term "transcendental" for Kant denotes the a priori factors in human knowledge. Maréchal read Thomas Aquinas in terms of this insight regarding the necessary a priori conditions of our cognition of objects. Rahner, from within this tradition of transcendental Thomism, concludes that it is in the transcendental experience, necessary for all human knowing, that the human being comes to know God.

Rahner argues that the human being is, by its very nature, a transcendental being. As such, the human being knows "God" as the infinite horizon of transcendence. To be a human being, or to have a human nature, is to have some sort of cognitive apprehension of the infinite ground of one's total experience. That the human being is open to God is self-evident, according to Rahner; it is a matter that may be discovered by the use of human reason. Rahner expounds his understanding of "grace" in the context of this understanding of human "nature" as open to its transcendent ground. Grace, for Rahner, is the self-gift of God in Jesus Christ. Grace is a matter of faith, yet Rahner's account of grace is always framed within an account of human knowledge of God, established independently of revelation. Conversely, there is no human nature that is "purely natural" in the sense of not having been graced, because God has really given God's self in revelation.

Rahner observes that if the human understanding of God derived only from that which can be discovered by human reason, without the aid of revelation, religion would be merely "natural religion," for example, the worship of nature as divine.[5] There is an interesting overlap between this observation and Schleiermacher's to the effect that without redemption there would be only the impulse toward God and not the possibility of that impulse being satisfied. However, just as for Schleiermacher there has been a redemption, so for Rahner there has been revelation. There is not only "natural" religion; there is also "supernatural religion." God genuinely gives God's self in such a way as to be received, without ceasing to be God.[6]

As Rahner ponders the implications of the reality of God's self-gift, he notes that if God really gives God's self, there also must be given the capacity for the gift to be received. This capacity Rahner terms the "supernatural existential." Both Rahner and Schleiermacher envisage a philosophical situation in which the human being *as human being* is conscious of itself as absolutely dependent upon an "other" for existence itself. In this situation the human being is characterized by an impulse toward—a reaching out for—that other. For both theologians, this situation would obtain independently of Jesus Christ; and for both, this impulse, or this reaching out, is distinguished from the capacity to receive the knowledge of God that has been gained in what Schleiermacher terms the redemption and Rahner calls the self-gift of God.

The Mediation of Knowledge

Rahner begins *Spirit in the World* with the unequivocal assertion that there is no such thing as an "intellectual intuition" of God, and he devotes the whole of the rest of the book to a defense of this claim. By denying that there can be an "intellectual intuition" of God, Rahner means precisely that there is no knowledge of God that is not mediated by the finite. Rahner reaches this conclusion through a detailed interpretation of Thomas's question in the *Summa Theologiae:* "Can the intellect actually know anything through the intelligible species which it possesses, without turning to the phantasms?" (q. 84, a. 7).

The "intelligible species" in this context refers to the "intellectual or abstract aspect of anything known."[7] The "phantasm" is the species that is evoked by the intellect from a thing's image. Thus, when the person is confronted with the thing, the phantasm is the idea that arises in the mind of the sort or the kind of that thing. Hence the phantasm derives from the imagination. Thomas's *quaestio* is whether the intellect can know anything, through an abstract or metaphysical knowledge, that is not based on ideas (phantasms) that derive from things.[8] (This is precisely the question that concerns Thiemann, though he formulates it differently. Thiemann asks whether there is an intuitive foundational knowing which is not mediated by the material world, and his reply—like that of Thomas and, as we shall see, Rahner—is a "no.")

Thomas, therefore, is asking a question about abstract ideas or metaphysical knowledge. Can there be abstract ideas which do not arise from confrontation with a thing? Can the intellect know anything on its own, that is, without the involvement of the *imaginatio*? For this to be the case the intellect would need to have its own "intuition" rather than relying on the processes of the imagination. It would involve an "immediate grasp in knowledge." So the question is, Does the intellect have its own intuition? Can the intellect know anything directly and immediately, that is to say apart from ideas which derive from things?

Thomas Aquinas in fact asks two questions: whether the human intellect can know the metaphysical at all, and whether it can know metaphysical reality independently of the *imaginatio*. In answer to the first, Thomas, according to Rahner, concludes that it can: there is a human metaphysics "which transcends everything spatial and temporal, encompasses all being absolutely, and reaches the absolute and the absolutely necessary."[9] In answer to the second, Thomas concludes that we cannot. Concurring with Aristotle, he argues that in the present state of life, while the intellect "is united with receptive corporeality," it is impossible to know anything without turning to the phantasms.[10]

While Rahner takes for granted the first conclusion, that the human intellect can know the metaphysical, he examines in some detail the second question: whether the intellect can know metaphysical reality independently of the *imaginatio*, that is, whether the intellect can know anything through a process which bypasses the human experience of the material world. Rahner first concludes with Thomas that such knowledge is not possible and then goes on to ask how the intellect can know that which is separated from all senses, when the only knowledge it has comes through the senses. Later in this chapter we return to the answer that Rahner gives to this question. For now, the most important point is that in *Spirit in the World*, Rahner expressly rejects the idea that there can be a knowledge of God which is not mediated by the finite world.

Rahner repeats this rejection in the first chapter of *Hearer of the Word*, where he argues that there is a meta-knowledge or "first knowledge" identical with metaphysics in the Aristotelian sense, and a "second knowledge" of engagement with external reality.

> [T]here is only *one* philosophical foundation for all sciences. Aristotle had already remarked this in the fourth book (Chapters I and IV) of the *Metaphysics*. Hence there exists one branch of knowledge which assigns their objects to the various sciences, determines the structure of this object, as presupposed by each science, provides the formal principles of knowledge deriving from this structure, and shows how the existence and the diversity of the sciences follows necessarily from the very fact that they are a human activity. The traditional name of this *epistéme próte* (first science) is metaphysics. Hence the statement: every problem of the philosophy of science is a problem of the one first science, metaphysics.
>
> Thus we see that the diversity of the sciences is based on a single, still mysterious ground, which determines their object, their function,

and their differences, and that the problem of the relation between two sciences is a metaphysical problem. This does not simply mean that metaphysics may occasionally reflect on the relation existing between two sciences. It means that she herself has originally established this relation, because, as first *epistéme,* she herself gives rise to these sciences. The multiplicity of the sciences must grow out of this one single ground of metaphysics. Therefore the problem of the relation between two sciences does not come up only after they have already been established: it is the problem of the bond that connects them in their common metaphysical ground.[11]

There is no access to "first knowledge" independent of "second knowledge." There can be no philosophical knowledge without knowledge of the finite, because all knowledge relies on the connection to a common ground of a metaphysical apprehension and an apprehension of the finite. Thus there is no knowledge at all without engagement with the material world.

Despite Rahner's unambiguous position on the mediation of knowledge in these early works, there are nonetheless two issues to be explored: first, whether, particularly in the more dense passages of his work, Rahner inadvertently contradicts his own position; second, whether, in spite of his efforts, his religious epistemology as it develops is in fact based on an underlying assumption that there can be a knowledge of God which is not mediated by the finite. With respect to the latter, Fergus Kerr's early criticism is perhaps the most damaging: "there surely is a *prima facie* case for suggesting that Rahner's most characteristic theological profundities are embedded in an extremely mentalist-individualist epistemology of unmistakably Cartesian provenance. Central to his whole theology, that is to say, is the possibility for the individual to occupy a standpoint beyond his immersion in the bodily, the historical and the institutional."[12]

Criticism such as this must be taken seriously, even though Kerr himself later rescinded his remarks.[13] Rahner's writings on religious epistemology contain passages that are difficult to reconcile. It is important to defend the claim that, while Rahner's description of the epistemological process at times is confusing, it is not "mentalist-individualist"; and further, Rahner is quite clear overall that knowledge of God is always mediated through concrete human experiences. For Rahner, the human being is a *historical* being precisely in having the power to reach out beyond the material world and know God.

The most problematic area of Rahner's epistemology centers on what, in one of the most difficult passages from the introduction to *Foundations of Christian Faith,* he terms "unthematic self-consciousness." Rahner argues that one experiences reality by possessing oneself and one's reflection in knowledge, and it is through this possession that one is spiritual. Spiritual knowledge is a knowledge in which the knowing subject possesses in knowledge both itself and its knowledge. In knowledge, not only is something known, but the subject's knowledge is always co-known. Self-consciousness is therefore always a consciousness of the subject's self which includes consciousness of the subject's knowledge.[14] Thus, Rahner concludes, it is by being aware of oneself and one's knowledge in the act of knowledge that one experiences God.

It is difficult to know what Rahner means here. He evidently intends that it is as a cognitive subject that one experiences God, and he takes the cognitive subject as the starting point for epistemology. The danger in taking the cognitive subject as the starting point, rather than, for example, language or action, conversation or collaboration, as Kerr suggests,[15] is that then one may be committed to the view that the individual works out his or her own salvation in isolated mental activity, without reference to the material world or to the community. The question arises, therefore, whether Rahner envisages an experience of God or a knowledge of God that is prelinguistic. The idea of a wordless encounter with God might seem to come straight from the Christian mystical tradition. Since Wittgenstein's work on the connection between experience and language, however, the idea that there can be a pre-linguistic experience of God is widely regarded as unacceptable.[16]

Rahner states that in the transcendental experience, the One whom we call "God" encounters the human person in silence. It is as the absolute and incomprehensible, as the term of human transcendence "which cannot really be incorporated into any system of coordinates," that God encounters the human person.[17] The silence is on both sides. The word "God" is the final word before "we become silent."[18] Rahner seems to dispense at this point with the use of language in the transcendental experience of God—but how is this "silence before God" to be interpreted? Are we talking here of a prelinguistic or nonconceptual experience of God? In discussing the transforming effect of the experience of God, Philip Endean answers as follows:

> The idea of God's action somehow transforming the subjectivity through which we experience all phenomena, altering the self's sense of its own identity, seems unobjectionable, indeed helpful and suggestive. The supposition that this process is "non-conceptual" seems at best ambiguous and at worst wrong-headed.... Obviously, God's otherness lies, as Hopkins puts it, "past all grasp"; and the supernatural existential is a transcendental reality which as such cannot simply be read off from external historical data. But neither of those self-evident points commits us to the incoherence of *saying* that God's action lies beyond the realm of *language*.[19]

Yet Endean recognizes the limitations of Rahner's account of human transcendence. Endean comments that Rahner's theological formulations are "focused simply on the material, bodily, and sensory aspects of the human," to the detriment of "language, culture and tradition." The result is a correspondingly limited account "of human experience, of human identity, of what Rahner called human transcendence."[20] Rahner might have provided a more satisfactory account of human transcendence had he come into contact with the later works of Wittgenstein, and indeed Endean goes on to develop an interpretation of Rahner's epistemology in terms of Wittgenstein's concept of "stage-setting."[21]

As it is, Rahner seems to be in danger of endorsing a position in which metaphysical knowledge is achieved independently of the senses—precisely the idea of an intellectual intuition which he specifically rejects in *Spirit in the World*. However, it is also evident in his writings that Rahner's intention is not to suggest that language has no role to play in the transcendental experience of God. For example, in commenting both on the rationalist position that reality is present only through the objectifying concept (*durch den vergegenständlichenden Begriff*) and the "modernist" position that reality is present through self-consciousness to the exclusion of the objectifying concept, Rahner states: "But there is not just the purely objective 'in itself' of a reality on the one hand, and the 'clear and distinct idea' of it on the other, but there is also a more original unity, not indeed for everything and anything, but certainly for the actualization of human existence, and this is a unity of reality and its 'self-presence' which is more, and is more original than the unity of this reality and the concept which objectifies it." In discussing this "original unity," Rahner argues that even in "original knowledge itself" there is a moment of reflection and therefore communicability: "This original unity which we are driving at between reality and its knowledge of itself always exists in man only with and in and through what we call language, and thus also reflection and communicability. At the moment when this element of reflection would no longer be present, this original self-possession would also cease to exist."[22] This "original unity," this knowledge to which the intellect most immediately has access, is possible only through language.

Furthermore, in both his earlier and later writings, Rahner clearly holds that knowledge of God is always mediated through concrete human experiences. According to Rahner, the experience of God is necessarily mediated by the linguistic tradition, or language in its broadest sense. Rahner would not want to suggest that a person can arrive at an experience of God somehow apart from that person's immersion in a particular historical tradition. Admittedly, the fact that Rahner seems to suggest a wordless encounter with God indicates an underdeveloped understanding of the connection between experience and language. It is true that Rahner discusses God's revelation in relation to the individual. It would be a mistake, however, to conclude that for Rahner, an individual can experience God or work out his or her own salvation in isolation. Rahner's understanding of the role of language in epistemology may be deficient or underdeveloped. Nonetheless, he shows signs of recognizing that the experience of existence and therefore of God occurs only within a given common language. Certainly his substantive position may be developed more fully in this direction.

Language and the Word "God"

As Rahner examines how, in practice, the human experience of God occurs, he looks at the word "God," as it inescapably occurs in our language. He argues that because there is such a word, translatable as "God," in every language, none of us can avoid the concept of God as the absolute mystery that grounds our existence. Yet more than that, Rahner is claiming that it is a necessary word for us. It is the word "God" that brings the human being "face to face with the single whole of reality . . . with the single whole of his own existence."[23] Rahner is claiming that anything which counts as a *human* language must have a word for God in it.[24] The word "God" is absolutely necessary for a language to be a *human* language.[25]

According to Rahner, the word "God" is the totality which grounds all the individual things we can name. "God" is not just any word, but is the word in which language grasps itself in its ground. No human language is explicable in itself; it relies for its meaning on a reference to the meaning of the single whole of reality, to which the human being is open as a transcendent creature. Without this reference to the single whole of reality, language could not exist.[26]

The word "God" functions like a proper name and says nothing more about God. The form of the word "reflects what the word refers to: the 'ineffable one,' the 'nameless one' who does not enter into the world we can name as a part of it."[27] God is therefore known only as the ground of the material world, and therefore *only through the material world*. The experience of God occurs within a given common language. Our formulated experience of reality is community-dependent. This is not a question of an individual's isolated experience of God.

Rahner's anthropology presents the human being—the being who is conscious of itself and its transcendence—as a necessarily historical being. In *Hearer of the Word*, Rahner stresses the historicity of the human person. Human persons are "essentially historical beings, who have to listen (to God) for a possible revelation."[28] Precisely as a creature who is transcendent, who has the power to reach out beyond the material world and know God, the human being is at the same time a *historical* being: "Even as spirit and precisely as spirit the human person is a *historical* being. Hence it is not only in our biological existence, but also for the very foundation of our spiritual existence, that we have to turn toward history."[29]

For Rahner, mere biological existence involves no sense of past or of a future goal. The *human* being is the being immersed in history, who *becomes* human in the course of a historical existence. This applies both to Jesus Christ, the archetypal human being and the climax of God's self-gift to humanity, and to all human beings as a result of their relationship to Christ.[30] Salvation, for Rahner, means the self-gift of God, offered and accepted, in Jesus Christ. And it is the salvation of the whole person, historically constituted, which takes place as the human being is "involved in history."[31]

> But if eschatological thought is concerned with *salvation*, and salvation is the fulfilment of the *whole* man and not just of some dimensions, then the thought of the fulfilment of certain elements, or better, the fulfilment of the one man under all aspects of his single, total and yet plural reality, cannot be absent.... The reference to a real future yet to come, involving all the aspects of man's being, may be omitted; or it may be eliminated in favour of an existential actualism in the course of an ostensible "de-mythization"; or it may be forgotten that man has a physical, spatio-temporal, bodily existence, even in matters of salvation.... But if so, man and his self-understanding have been really mythologized, because his linear direction in time towards what is still to come in time, and hence the dimension of his historicity, has been omitted. And since it is there that he works out his salvation with his God, his salvation would not take place where we really are.[32]

For Rahner, therefore, God's self-gift in revelation is mediated in the transcendental experience according to the particular circumstances of the subject's historical existence. Various individual experiences will mediate knowledge of God with more "clarity and persuasiveness" than others, and will "vary a great deal from person to person." These experiences serve to make the individual person aware of the fact that the experience of transcendence takes place repeatedly, without necessarily being recognized as such, in "the immediate involvement with the concrete world."[33]

God as a Permanent Accompaniment to All Human Experience

For Schleiermacher, as we have seen, the experience of absolute dependence, or the experience of God, takes place in our awareness of limited dependency on the world. It is now necessary to locate the experience of God in Rahner's approach and to see exactly how, for him, the experience of God takes place in the experience of the finite.

Having unequivocally rejected the notion of an "intellectual intuition" of God, as we have seen, Rahner seeks nonetheless to demonstrate that the finite intellect can know that which transcends the finite. Rahner asks, What determines the relationship between our cognitive power—consisting of both the intellect and the imagination—and its object? He argues that neither intellect nor imagination can be active without an "objectification." In particular, for the intellect to be able to form abstract concepts an objectification must take place. And for this objectification to occur, according to Rahner, the intellect must reach beyond the field of the imagination. Thus this objectification requires a prior knowledge that cannot be supplied by sensible intuition. But since there is no intellectual intuition, where is this prior knowledge to come from?

In *Spirit in the World*, Rahner here appeals to the concept of *excessus* borrowed from Thomas Aquinas. For Thomas, the *excessus* is a knowledge that exceeds the thing that is given to the senses when a particular thing is known through the senses. The universal concept produced when something is objectified goes well beyond knowledge of the thing known, and it is this going beyond that he terms the *excessus*. For Thomas, according to Rahner, this reaching beyond the imagination is a metaphysical act in that it is an apprehension of a universal concept: thereby, a reality outside the dimensions of space and time is apprehended for the first time. This *excessus*, this knowledge that exceeds knowledge of the intuited thing, cannot be an intellectual intuition, however, since a "reaching beyond" cannot at the same time be an "immediate grasp in knowledge." Rather, the *excessus* is the precondition for objectification, which is a precondition for the knowledge of the imagination. As Rahner explains, "[W]e would not go beyond the scope of the Thomistic problematic by considering the *excessus* not as something which comes subsequently to the experience of world, but as the very condition of the possibility of the experience of world. . . . The *excessus* to metaphysics, which takes place in a conversion to the phantasm, is considered as a condition of the truth of knowledge of world."[34]

Rahner thus interprets this notion of *excessus* as a transcendent reaching beyond the field of the imagination and deems it to be the fundamental act of knowledge, the precondition for our knowledge of the finite world. Thomas Aquinas had pointed to the intellect's capacity to go beyond sensory perception. Rahner takes this further and speaks of an infinite "going beyond," which serves as the background to the cognitive process as a whole. On Rahner's analysis, human knowing is a power that reaches out beyond the reality accessible in a concrete way to human experience and knows the metaphysical.

The corporeal thing can only be objectified against that which surrounds or delimits it. In other words, Rahner argues, it can only be objectified against some sort of background. The background itself cannot be intuited, since it must be prior to the objectifying intuition. Thus, when the thing is intuited, an apprehension necessarily takes place that goes beyond the thing intuited, beyond the field of the imagination to the ground of knowing. For Rahner, God is known in an original way (*ursprünglich*) in the act of knowing as such, as the infinite ground that makes possible knowledge of the finite. "[T]o know God as the ground of the existent does not mean: to know that God (as already known beforehand) is the ground of the thing, but: to know that the ground, already and always opened simultaneously in knowing the existent being, is the Absolute Being, that is, God, and thus to know God for the first time."[35]

It follows that God, for Rahner, is a permanent accompaniment to all human experience. God, on this interpretation, is present in human conscious activity as such, as the precondition for all human knowing. Rahner's philosophical position on this matter was already worked out by 1936, when *Spirit in the World* was submitted as a doctoral thesis. Forty years later, Rahner was still expounding this view in *Foundations*.

The original knowledge of God, Rahner maintains, has the character of a transcendental experience.[36] God is the infinite reference or ground of the finite which makes possible the objectification of the finite in the experience of transcendence. Thus, Rahner presents an image of the human spirit reaching beyond the object to the infinite ground as the thing is objectified. In logical order (but simultaneously in time), there is activity of the spirit, consciousness of the infinite ground, and consciousness of the thing. Consciousness of the infinite ground is a consciousness of God.

> It is self-evident that this transcendental experience of human transcendence is not the experience of some definite, particular objective thing [*Gegenständlichen*] which is experienced alongside of other objects [*Gegenständen*]. It is rather a basic mode of being which is prior to and permeates every objective experience [*gegenständlichen Erfahrung*]. We must emphasize again and again that the transcendence meant here is not the thematically conceptualized 'concept' of transcendence in which transcendence is reflected upon objectively [*gegenständlich*]. It is rather the a priori openness of the subject to being as such, which is present precisely when a person experiences himself as involved in the multiplicity of cares and concerns and fears and hopes of his everyday world. Real transcendence is always in the background, so to speak, in those origins of human life and human knowledge over which we have no control.[37]

It is the permanent background experience to all experience of the finite. It is not something that comes and goes with isolated experiences, but the permanent condition of all conscious activity. The fact that human knowledge of the infinite and human knowledge of the finite are distinct, and yet neither can exist without the other, means that knowledge of God, as the transcendent ground of the finite, is an ever-present reality for the human being.

Arguments for God's Existence

For Schleiermacher, proofs for the existence of God have been superseded by a recognition of the universality of the consciousness of God in the consciousness of oneself as absolutely dependent. In Rahner's strategy there is a similar inevitability in positing God's existence. God necessarily exists as the condition for human knowing and *human* being. What grounds human openness, what grounds the reaching out in the unlimited expanse of human transcendence, cannot be nothingness, since that would make no sense. As the infinite horizon of human transcendence, God necessarily exists. Rahner first sets out this argument in *Hearer of the Word* in relation to the concept of *Vorgriff*, by which, rather than the term *excessus*, he refers to the "more," in the "reaching for more" (*auf mehr ausgreifenden Vorgang*) that is involved in grasping an individual object of the senses (*sinnlich gegebene Dieses*).[38] If transcendence, in Rahner's sense, is not illusory, then "this 'more' can only be the absolute range of all knowable objects as such" (*die absolute Weite der erkennbaren Gegenständ*), and necessarily exists if human beings are transcendent beings.[39]

In a brief passage in chapter 5 of *Hearer of the Word*, Rahner sets this necessary existence of God within the broad context of the ontological argument. He reformulates the question about being to provoke the response that necessarily affirms God's existence. Thus, "Since being itself (therefore, God) is intrinsically intelligible, does the human being have the capacity to receive the intelligibility of God?" becomes, "On what basis does the reaching out after knowledge transcend the single object that knowledge captures?" (*worauf transzendiert das menschliche vorgreifende Erkennen in der Erfassung seines Einzelobjektes?*).[40] The reformulation is a question about the infinite ground that makes knowledge possible. Rahner then reformulates the Scholastic answer: "[T]he range of the *Vorgriff* extends toward being as such, with no inner limit in itself, and therefore includes also the absolute being of God."[41] When the question is asked about the infinite ground that makes possible knowledge of the finite, then the existence of the infinite ground is necessarily affirmed. Since knowing does not deny but affirms existence, that which grounds the finite object in the act of knowing cannot be nothingness. It can only be absolute being.

The notion of the infinite ground of human transcendence and the idea of "reaching" in knowledge after a more that is always more than one can reach, reflect the pattern of the ontological argument, namely, of persistently attempting to think that which is always beyond the reaches of thought. However, by taking the knowing of the single finite object as the context within which God's existence is affirmed, Rahner claims to treat the argument as an a posteriori argument rather than an a priori one: "This is by no means an *a priori* demonstration of God, like that of Augustine, derived from the 'eternal truths,' or like that of Anselm or of

Leibniz. The *Vorgriff* and its range, as the always present and necessary condition of all knowledge, can be known and affirmed only in the *a posteriori* knowledge of a real being and as the necessary condition of that knowledge."[42] It is not an a priori argument because it is based on the experience of the finite world. For Rahner, there can be no valid argument for the existence of God that is not based on experience of the finite world. Rahner's position is more akin to a cosmological argument, insofar as he asserts the necessity for some sort of explanation for the phenomena given in experience.

Rahner's strategy, therefore, is to take a concept for which he hopes to elicit general agreement—the necessary infinite ground of human knowing—and to call that "God." Once Rahner has elicited agreement on the concept, those in agreement must concede the existence of God. Rahner, as we have seen, argues that for a language to be a *human* language it must have in it a word for "God" as the infinite ground of human transcendence, or the infinite ground of being itself. And as that infinite ground, "God" self-evidently exists.

The inevitability of positing God's existence whenever one reflects upon human existence is a constant theme for Rahner. For example, in chapter 3 of *Hearer of the Word,* he says, "We cannot abstain from answering the question about being; an answer is always forthcoming, because the question belongs always and necessarily to our existence. Always and of necessity we posit in our existence the 'whence' for an answer, hence implicitly the answer to the question of being itself."[43] Rahner's lack of interest in the individual classical arguments for God's existence can be explained, in short, by this inevitability. All the proofs, he remarks later in *Foundations,* "be they cosmological, theological, kinetic, axiological, deontological, noetic or moral proofs," are but different expressions of the one proof.[44] All proofs take certain categorical realities and attempt to understand them, only to find that those realities can only be understood or known through interpretation, in the act of transcendence. That the transcendental ground of the thing known, disclosed in the act of knowing, is necessary for the knowledge of the categorical reality to take place at all, means that the very act of knowing a categorical reality itself has a guaranteed referent. Since the thing is known, the referent necessary for the thing to be known exists.

For both Rahner and Schleiermacher, the traditional arguments for God's existence are superseded. Whatever form these arguments take, they can be reduced to a single argument, drawn from the recognition of the universality of the consciousness of God in the consciousness of oneself as absolutely dependent (Schleiermacher), or drawn from the recognition of the necessity of the transcendental ground as the condition of human knowing (Rahner). That Schleiermacher and Rahner each give a different account of the argument does not imply that either one is mistaken or there are two distinct arguments. Schleiermacher's "evidence" for God's existence, which lies in an analysis of the consciousness of the self, and Rahner's "evidence," which lies in an analysis of the act of knowing any finite reality (including the self), are basically equivalent arguments. A proper analysis of human being necessarily posits God as its transcendental ground.

Philosophy and Theology

Central to the present study is the contention that there are certain similarities between Schleiermacher's and Rahner's religious epistemologies. Moreover, just as Schleiermacher's theology had to be defended against the charge of foundationalism, the claim that Rahner's theology is foundationalist demands similar attention. Various interpreters of Rahner have put forward such a claim. Karen Kilby describes its most common form: "[I]t is often suggested or assumed that in Rahner one finds a Roman Catholic example of a typically modern and liberal foundationalist approach to theology, whereby an appeal is made to a purportedly universal pre-thematic religious experience ('transcendental experience' in Rahner's case) and this is used to legitimate and give meaning to the whole edifice of the Christian faith."[45] In the view of such critics, the similarities between Rahner and Schleiermacher would only serve to demonstrate that Rahner's thinking is as flawed as Schleiermacher's. Kilby also points to another group of theologians, serious readers of Rahner, who do not think that Rahner's "theology can simply be read off of or mechanically deduced from the philosophy," but who nonetheless "do presume that the philosophy plays a major role as support for the theology . . . [who]

believe, in other words, that the theology is logically dependent on the philosophy, even if it is not simplistically determined by it."[46] Kilby describes this type of reading as semi-foundationalist.[47]

The defense of Rahner's religious epistemology that has been given up to this point has followed a similar pattern to the defense of Schleiermacher. The aim has been to demonstrate that on balance, in spite of some troublesome passages, Rahner plainly views the knowledge of God as always historically and culturally mediated. It is not merely the construct of the Cartesian ego. Rahner's theology cannot "simply be read off or mechanically deduced" from his philosophy. This disposes of the most common form of the foundationalist charge. What remains to be determined is whether it is possible to defend Rahner against the charge of a less blatant form of foundationalism.

Kilby is of the opinion that a nonfoundationalist interpretation of Rahner's theology is impossible as long as his later theology is tied to his earlier philosophy. What is at issue here is the legitimate relationship between theology and philosophy. For Kilby, "Rahner's theology can be read—and indeed, . . . it is *best* read—nonfoundationally. That is to say . . . his theology is best understood as logically independent of his philosophy." The widespread assumption, says Kilby, is that Rahner's philosophy provides a "support" for his theology.[48] In her view, although his philosophy does not determine his theology in the simplistic fashion that is claimed by at least some of his commentators, it does inevitably appear to contribute to the theology in a manner that is unacceptable. To some extent his theology is *founded* on his philosophy, rather than deriving solely from revelation.

What follows in this section is intended to counter the view that Rahner's theology is best understood as logically independent of his philosophy. The aim is to demonstrate that Rahner's philosophy plays a necessary role in his theological interpretation, yet one which does not presume to determine the content of revelation that is the subject matter of the theological enterprise. This distinction is, or should be, the one at issue in the various discussions centering on whether Rahner is a foundationalist. We have seen that Thiemann defined foundationalism in such a wide sense that his own theological construction could be deemed foundationalist. In assessing Kilby's discussions of Rahner, one must ask whether, on her reading, *any* philosophical grounding of theology is intrinsically foundationalist.

Rahner's philosophy and theology are intimately linked throughout his writings. The philosophy performs two functions, both of which contribute to theology in a necessary way. The task of theology is to articulate the content of revelation, and philosophy is an essential tool, without which the task would be impossible. Necessarily, philosophy influences the articulation, since providing the means whereby theology may be articulated is its first function. Philosophy is a precondition for any expression, even for any understanding, of what revelation teaches. Without some basic philosophical concept of "evil" or "morality" or "love" or "God," there would be no mechanism for the message of the Gospel to be appropriated.[49] On this account, Rahner's philosophy may be said to determine the expression of revelation, but it does not follow that his philosophy determines its content.

Philosophy's second function is to provide some sort of justification, some sort of evidence which can be called upon in support of specific religious beliefs. But what sort of justification? This is a critical issue. What sort of evidence does philosophy provide? What precisely is it that philosophy provides evidence *for*? Emphatically, philosophy does not provide evidence for the *truth* of what Christians believe. There can be no question of the justification of faith in terms of proving to be true that which one believes through faith. It is only the *rationality* of believing what one believes that can be justified. Thus what is not claimed for Christian apologetics, or at least what should not be claimed, is the ability to prove that what revelation teaches about the God/world relationship is true. It can only demonstrate that to believe what is taught is not an irrational thing to do.

Turning to Rahner's philosophical concept of God, it is possible to see how the two functions of philosophy work out in practice. However, it is first necessary to clarify the use of "concept of God" in this context. Rahner's "God," as we have seen, is the name of what answers the questions about the ultimate; it is the word that functions like a proper name and says nothing more about God. Rahner describes the experience of God in terms of the rather troublesome notion of the "unthematic self-consciousness" and talks of a precondition of knowing using the virtually untranslatable word *Vorgriff*.[50] In considering what Rahner has to say about the *Vorgriff* in *Hearer of the Word*, the connotations of incompletion or emptiness in his description of the experience of God are striking. "The *Vorgriff* and its range," he says, "as the always present and necessary condition of all knowledge, can be known and affirmed only in the *a posteriori* knowledge of a real being and as the necessary condition of that knowledge."[51] The reaching out of the human spirit in the transcendental experience is an emptiness that remains to be filled by contact with the finite world. However, since it never exists apart from such contact, it might perhaps be described as a "filled emptiness."

All of these remarks should serve to ensure that when we talk of Rahner's philosophical "concept" of God, we do so only on the understanding that this is to a large degree an "empty" concept. There is a strong sense in which this concept has yet to be filled out with content.

Rahner's philosophical concept of God succeeds in performing both of the functions of philosophy mentioned above. In the first instance it enables Rahner to articulate his faith. His philosophy provides the basic philosophical concept of God that is necessary before one can claim, for example, that God is love. It is not the case, however, that Rahner's specific elaboration on the philosophical concept is essential to faith. Thus, when he says that the word "God" is the word that human beings use to describe the infinite horizon of human transcendence, he is emphatically not saying that anyone who takes issue with the words "infinite," "horizon," or "transcendence" lacks the philosophical concept of God that is necessary for Christian faith. On the contrary, Rahner claims that every person, insofar as he or she is a human being, has the necessary philosophical concept of "God" that equates to what Rahner himself describes as the infinite horizon of human transcendence. "God" is the word for the mystery that grounds human existence. It is a word that is unavoidable for human beings, because human existence is not self-explanatory. Whatever word it is that anyone uses for the mystery of existence, the concept implied by that word is what Rahner is talking about when he uses the word "God." Even the person who says, "I do not believe in God," possesses the philosophical concept of God that for a self-conscious human being is unavoidable.

Confusion can arise when "God" as a philosophical concept is mixed up with that in which Rahner believes by faith. In distinguishing between the two, we must bear in mind that even if there is a clear distinction between the philosophical concept and the theological expression, the philosophical concept itself is always tinged with the effects of revelation. Even if Rahner wanted to do so, he could not simply, completely, step outside his faith context. The implications of this fact can be explored by considering a criticism of David Burrell, which challenges the type of argument that Rahner employs to arrive at the conclusion that the existence of God is self-evident.

Rahner treats the question to which the answer is "God" as a *philosophical* question. Burrell, on the other hand, claims that "the apparently spontaneous enquiry: whence did all this come?" is a question asked from the point of view of faith. He argues that the Judeo-Christian tradition has reversed a mindset more natural to human inquiry, one that presumes the universe is simply "there."[52] Burrell thus directly challenges the philosophical grounding of Rahner's theology. Yet such a claim need not disturb our initial findings, provided two things are borne in mind. In the first place, no philosophical claim can be purely philosophical if God's grace is operative in the world; but this does not make it impossible to identify a philosophical claim and distinguish it from one that is theological. Second, the fact that a philosophical claim is challenged need not be a cause for concern, since while Rahner (necessarily) expresses his faith in terms of his own philosophical understanding, his appeal to pluralism means that other interpretations, based on different philosophical outlooks, are not ruled out. Thus, even for those who might agree with Burrell's comment, it is safe to say, for the purposes of differentiating Rahner's philosophy and his theology, that Rahner's concept of God as a "name," which says nothing more about that which is named, belongs squarely in Rahner's philosophy, along with other concepts that can be deduced from human reflection on the phenomena of experience. This concept is not what he believes in by faith.

What Rahner believes is that God has given God's own self to human beings in love. There is nothing self-evident about this belief. There can be no question of proving this belief to be true. However, the philosophical concept of God does allow Rahner to defend such a belief against the objection that *any* talk of God is nonsensical. When it comes to theological truth claims, it is only the rationality of believing such claims that can be defended, not the truth of the claims themselves. And for such a defense it is necessary to employ the philosophical concept of God, as well as other philosophical concepts such as "human being" and "love."

Thus, Rahner's earlier philosophy need not be set aside to prevent the corruption of his theology by inappropriate philosophical input. Instead, rigorous attention must be paid to what precisely Rahner thinks he can and cannot prove, and what precisely he thinks is self-evident. In the above example, we must respect the strictly philosophical status of his concept of God and the fact that this concept, which for Rahner is self-evident, is, as it were, empty of any faith content. When the concept is filled out with faith content, Rahner's philosophy will influence the interpretation of the faith content.

CHAPTER 6

An Alternative Approach

We now arrive at the question of how Rahner and Schleiermacher understand the relationship between God and the world. It is already evident that neither treats the world and God as parallel realities. Each in his different way has described the consciousness of God as the permanent background to human conscious experience. Rahner has explicitly stated that transcendental experience is not the experience of some objective thing, experienced alongside other objects. Schleiermacher has likewise made it clear, in his discussion of the human experience of limited freedom in relation to the world and of *absolute* dependence upon God, that the divine and the human cannot be depicted as the same *kind* of reality. If Rahner and Schleiermacher are able to explain the relationship between God and the world in a way that respects their infinite difference, they will succeed, where Swinburne and the postliberal theologians studied here have failed, in upholding the notion of God's "transcendence." In addressing the relationship of God and the world in their theologies, it is necessary first to discuss the way in which God's transcendence should be understood.

Creation and God's Transcendence

We have seen that Thiemann, in line with the Lutheran tradition, is primarily concerned to uphold the notion of God's transcendence.

Thiemann argues that the notion that God operates on the world from without—what he terms the "causal model of revelation"—is incompatible with the Christian notion of human freedom and raises questions regarding the rationality of belief. Both Rahner and Schleiermacher clearly hold that God does not "operate on the world from without." Both also point out that the contrast frequently made between transcendence and "immanence" cannot be appropriate in talking about God.

Schleiermacher comments, for example, on the difference between a theist and a pantheist: "The distinction, always somewhat strange—I might even say crudely drawn—between a God who is outside or over the world and a God who is in the world, does not particularly coincide with—to say the least—the actual reality, because strictly speaking, with regard to God, nothing can be said in terms of a contrast between inner and outer without somehow jeopardizing the divine omnipotence and omnipresence."[1] The picture of a God who is outside or above the world, a picture that runs alongside the contrasting image of God as within the world, is inappropriate. Such parallel images also imply that God is "spatially" limited. Both, therefore, involve some sort of identification between God and the world.

Schleiermacher, as we have seen, made an effort to distance himself from pantheism in his later work. Yet he recognizes a value that underlies the pantheist position. For Schleiermacher, there *is* a sense in which there is an identification of the world with God. God cannot be thought of as the sum total of the created world, yet there must be an identification of some sort between God and the world, he believes, since the only alternative to identification is an unacceptable distinction.

Rahner says something similar. God is, for both Schleiermacher and Rahner, the "whence" or transcendent ground of human existence. For Rahner too, God's transcendence cannot be thought of "spatially." Rahner also rejects pantheism, which makes a straightforward identification between God and the world. Yet, like Schleiermacher, he sees in it "an element of truth."[2] Schleiermacher has argued that in rejecting pantheism, a distinction should not be made between a God who is outside the world and a God who is in the world. Setting aside the question of God's immanence, Rahner makes the point that God and the non-divine cannot be placed as simply two things alongside each other. The claim "that God and the world are different," Rahner observes, "is radically misunderstood if it is interpreted in a dualistic way."³ He states further:

> The difference between God and the world is of such a nature that God establishes and is the difference of the world from himself, and for this reason he establishes the closest unity precisely in the differentiation. For if the difference itself comes from God, and, if we can put it this way, is itself identical with God, then the difference between God and the world is to be understood quite differently than the difference between categorical realities. Their difference is antecedent to them because they presuppose as it were a space which contains and differentiates them, and no one of these categorically distinct realities itself establishes its difference from the other or is this difference.⁴

Rahner's use of the term "space" is significant here. God's transcendence cannot be thought of "spatially." Since "space" is where the differentiation between categorical realities takes place, it cannot be an appropriate concept in understanding the relation between God and the world. The doctrine of transcendence cannot imply that there is "space" between God and the world. In explaining what transcendence means, namely, that there is no "space" between God and the world, Rahner in fact also establishes an account of God's immanence.

The tantalizing notion that God establishes and is the difference between the world and God's own self is one that has recently been taken up by Robert Sokolowski, as he "seeks to discover an indication of the divine even in the materiality of the world."⁵ Rahner says that God establishes the closest unity with the world precisely in establishing the difference between God and the world. On the assumption that this difference is established in its most radical expression with the Incarnation, Sokolowski's thought appears to augment the understanding of otherness that Rahner is straining to define. Sokolowski remarks that "the doctrine of the incarnation implicitly tells us something about the nature of the divine. For the incarnation to be possible, the divine nature must not be conceived as one of the natures within the whole of the world. It must be conceived as so other to the world that the union in the incarnation would not be an incoherence."[6] The differentiation between God and that which is created cannot be the same differentiation that takes place between categorical realities.

God, for Rahner, is the infinite horizon of human transcendence, which is at the same time "the absolute ground of every particular existent."[7] It is on account of *this* understanding, worked out in the context of the relationship between God and the human being, that Rahner is able to interpret God as ontologically other. God's transcendence consists in an ontological otherness that cannot be differentiated in the way that otherness is differentiated between categorical realities. Thus, to contrast transcendence and immanence is already to imply an erroneous understanding of transcendence. Rather, there is an identification between God and finite reality. The identification *and the otherness* consist in the fact that God is the absolute ground of every existent.

It is evident that both Schleiermacher and Rahner intend their philosophy of God, which is set in the context of God's self-gift in grace or revelation, to portray God as transcendent yet immanent in creation, without making a distinction between God outside and God in the world. The key to their success in this matter lies in their understanding of the creator/creature relationship. Crucial here is their understanding of what it means to be creature, learned, one assumes, through their experience of the spiritual life. Their spiritual experience within the Christian tradition would have brought into sharp focus what they believe is a universal human experience, namely, the feeling of absolute dependence on the whence of existence, or the transcendental experience of God as the ground of one's being. The whence or ground of existence, that from which existence absolutely derives, is the creator.

God, for Schleiermacher, is the experienced whence of human existence. Through the consciousness of absolute dependence, which is a permanent human condition, the human being is in a permanent experienced relationship with God. God, for Rahner, is the transcendent ground of being, known in self-consciousness. Through the transcendental experience the human being is in a permanent experienced relationship with God. If the experience of the relationship with God as Schleiermacher and Rahner describe it were, as Thiemann says, an experience in which the human being is removed from the world of particular times, places, and so on, then Schleiermacher and Rahner would not have successfully demonstrated God's immanence. Yet for both, the immanence of God in creation is integral to their thinking. Schleiermacher's understanding of revelation introduces a stronger sense of divine presence than his strict philosophy of God, just as Rahner's reference to God's self-gift in grace introduces a stronger sense of divine presence than his philosophical argument alone. Yet this "stronger sense" falls within the philosophical framework that has been set out. All experience of God through grace/revelation is mediated through the material world as its ground. All that the doctrine of God's immanence can mean is that the created world mediates the presence of God. There is here, of course, no question of a distinction between God who is outside and God who is within the world.

Plainly, what enables Schleiermacher and Rahner to uphold both the doctrine of the transcendence of God and the doctrine of the immanence of God is their understanding of the creator/creature relationship. Conversely, I argue, what has prevented much modern theology from being true to both these doctrinal notions simultaneously is a misunderstanding of the creator/creature relationship—a misunderstanding amounting to a reduction of what it means for God to be creator and for human beings to be God's creation.

Swinburne, as I have shown, treats the phenomena of the created world as phenomena that require an ultimate explanation, and in doing so arrives at a notion of God. According to this notion, God is the one who, at some point in the past, has created the world but who remains outside it, so that the world has a God-given but separate existence. This view is confirmed in Swinburne's account of miracles: a miracle is God "intervening" in the world's events.[8] Thus creation, according to Swinburne's thinking, has a certain degree of independence vis-à-vis God. Even Thiemann's view of creation, though it contains no suggestion of human independence vis-à-vis God, is unsatisfactory.[9] To say that "causation might well describe God's original act of creation" is not in keeping with the notion of *creatio continua*.

Schleiermacher and Rahner, in marked contrast to Swinburne, place the absolute dependence of human beings on God at the center of their theologies. For Schleiermacher, there is no possibility of that which is created having a separate, albeit God-given, existence, since there is no possibility of any degree of independence on the part of the human being in relation to God. The absolute dependence of the human being upon God, for Scheiermacher, is such that it makes no sense to talk of God creating the world and God preserving the world in existence as two separate acts. We have artificially divided the notion of creation from the notion of preservation, but "there is no sufficient reason for retaining this division":[10]

> The proposition that the totality of finite being exists only in dependence upon the Infinite is the complete description of that basis of every religious feeling which is here to be set forth. We find ourselves always and only in a continuous existence . . . in whatever part of the whole or at whatever point of time we may be placed, in every full act of reflection we should recognize ourselves as thus involved in continuity. . . . The proposition that God sustains the world, considered in itself, is precisely similar. At least it only seems to have acquired another and lesser content because we have grown accustomed to think of preservation and creation together, and thus a beginning is excluded from the range of the idea of preservation. On the other hand, the proposition, "God has created," considered in itself, lays down absolute dependence, but only for the beginning, with the exclusion of development.[11]

The result of considering preservation and creation separately, as separate acts of God and as separate doctrines, is that each notion suffers a reduction. Creation is envisaged as though it did not involve God continually sustaining creation in existence; preservation is envisaged as though it began only after a certain point, the point when God brought forth the person or thing into existence. Although all things have not come into existence simultaneously, Schleiermacher can "find nothing the origin of which cannot be brought under the concept of preservation, so that the doctrine of creation is completely absorbed in the doctrine of preservation." Similarly, the "new beginnings" that make up the continued existence of individual created things "can be regarded as a creation," so that "the concept of creation if taken in its whole range makes the concept of preservation superfluous."[12]

If human beings, therefore, rely absolutely on God for their existence, then God's creative act is not a once and for all historical act, but an ongoing, ever-present act that maintains the human being in existence for as long as it exists. This insight enables Schleiermacher's theology to accommodate simultaneously the ideas of God's immanence and of God's transcendence. God is permanently mediated to the human being through the material world as the whence of human existence, yet as the whence of human existence, God is absolutely other.

Rahner, too, is quite clear that the creative act of God is an ongoing act. Like Schleiermacher, he understands creatureliness as a radical, ongoing dependence. The human being comes to know God through a transcendental experience, and God is known in that experience as its infinite ground. In that experience, "we experience what creatureliness is and we experience it immediately."[13]

> [W]hat it really means to have a created origin is experienced basically and originally in the process of transcendence. This means that in the first instance the terms "creatureliness," "being created" or "creation" do not point back to an earlier moment in time at which the creation of the creature in question once took place. They mean rather an ongoing and always actual process which for every existent is taking place now just as much as at an earlier point of time in his existence, although this ongoing creation is that of an existent extended *in time*. In the first instance, then, creation and creatureliness do not mean a momentary event, namely, the first moment of a temporal existent, but mean the establishing of this existent and his time itself, and this establishing does not enter into time, but is the ground of time.[14]

Significant here is the absolute closeness of the relationship between the creature and that which creates. The latter is the permanent "ground" of the former. The former exists and finds its identity only in the latter. This is true not merely at a particular point in time, when the creature receives its identity in a creative act never to be repeated, but permanently in an on-going creative act, for as long as the creature exists. "This radical dependence must be ongoing, and therefore not just affect the first moment, for what is finite is related now and always to the absolute as its ground."[15]

For Rahner the relationship between God and the world is not a variation on a relationship that can be found elsewhere, but is a unique relationship. How, then, is the relationship to be envisaged? The answer is surely that the human being—the creature—finds its identity in God as its permanent ground. This is the way, and the only way, in which the relationship can be understood. Divine immanence and divine transcendence, far from being in tension, are mutually entailed. The ontological otherness of God grounds the existence of the created world in such a way that the created world mediates the presence of God. Crucial to this understanding of God's transcendence and immanence is the notion of creatureliness, the notion of a dependence so absolute that creation must be interpreted as an ongoing event. Once the spatial connotations of "transcendence" and "immanence" are discounted, the appearance of tension between them is illusory.

Sokolowski again offers a way to explore further these intriguing ideas in the theologies of Schleiermacher and Rahner. Like Schleiermacher, Sokolowski also distinguishes between creation in a "narrow" sense, which must be supplemented by preservation, and "creation in a wider and fuller sense," which obviates the necessity for a doctrine of preservation.[16] Schleiermacher and Rahner uphold the notion of God's transcendence on the basis of what it means for God to be creator and for human beings to be God's creation. Sokolowski, in the same vein, arrives at a doctrine of creation as the locus where God's otherness can be determined. He regards his phenomenological theology of disclosure as a supplement to Scholastic theology: "Scholasticism reflected on the existence and nature of God, and on the world in its relation to God, but it carried out its work within the horizon set by the Christian distinction between the world and God. It did not examine the emergence of the distinction itself. It took the presence of the distinction for granted."[17] In a postmodern context, Sokolowski argues, theologians are in a position to examine the emergence of the distinction in the doctrine of creation. It is now possible to discuss creation "as that which defines how we are to understand God, how we are to understand the world, and how we are to understand the relationship between the world and God."[18]

Human Freedom

Once the creator/creature relationship has been properly understood, human freedom appears in a very different light from that which provoked Swinburne and Thiemann to some of their more extraordinary statements. Swinburne defends freedom as the freedom to assent to a probability; Thiemann defends it as the ability to give free intellectual assent to revelation. Both associate freedom in relation to God with the ability to act from a position of nescience.

Lindbeck, in contrast to Swinburne and Thiemann, clearly thinks that freedom in relation to God has wider implications than that of choosing to believe that something is true, implications which involve the whole being. He talks of a molding of one's life in such a way that it conforms to ultimate reality. Yet since he fails to recognize God as the ground of existence in Schleiermacher's and Rahner's sense—as "first cause" in a premodern, metaphysical sense—he too is blind to the reality of authentic human freedom. Authentic freedom is the freedom to give oneself over to the true ground of one's existence, rather than basing one's existence on a false ground in oneself.

Schleiermacher, as we have seen, clearly holds that we are never free in an absolute sense. While human beings have a limited feeling of freedom in relation to the world, this self-consciousness, according to Schleiermacher, "negatives absolute freedom."[19] We are never free in an absolute sense because "the whole of our spontaneous activity comes from a source outside of us."[20]

Is the human being always to be disappointed, then, by the limitations of the freedom at its disposal? Are human beings no freer than if God were to act upon them "from without?" As with the notion of God's transcendence, the notion of human freedom depends upon the interpretation of the notion of creatureliness—what it means to have being from another. If the human being seeks *absolute* freedom, if it seeks to deny its own creatureliness, it will always be disappointed. Since the human being as such is that which has being from another, authentic *human* freedom will only be found within the context of creatureliness.

Given that we have our being from another, from the whence of our existence, our freedom consists in the freedom to accept or reject that whence as the source of our being. The arena where this acceptance or rejection is played out is the historical world. In this setting of limited freedom, the choices we make are always at the same time a rejection or an acceptance of the whence as the source of being. Rahner, who, like Schleiermacher, recognizes that there is no absolute human freedom, also, like Schleiermacher, maintains that we cannot avoid making these choices. The whence of human existence, or God, is the infinite horizon of human transcendence. Just as there is no route to God outside the transcendental experience, so, since the human being is essentially a transcendent being, there is no avoiding a relationship with God, whether it be in terms of affirming or rejecting the relationship. The relationship itself, while it can be rejected, cannot be avoided. Although each of us can seek to sever the relationship with God, precisely as humans we cannot step outside the relationship, since we have our being from no other source, and since the world in which we are placed, and of which we must try to make sense, has no other ground. Thus every individual, precisely as a human being, whether it be through a rejection or through an acceptance of its creatureliness, necessarily takes some stance in relation to God.

The freedom which is available to us is, therefore, the freedom to accept or reject creatureliness. The only authentically human choice is for acceptance, since rejection would be a rejection of one's humanity. Authentic *human* freedom lies, therefore, in the acceptance of creatureliness. It lies in the affirmative stance that one takes up in relation to God, and it is in this free act of acceptance that a person knows God. The choice is made as one exercises one's limited freedom in relation to the world, in living through the particular circumstances of one's historical existence, which derive their meaning only in relation to God as their infinite ground.

The arena where the acceptance or rejection of creatureliness is played out is, as has been stated, the historical world. In this setting of limited freedom, the choices that are made are always at the same time a rejection or an acceptance of the whence as the source of being. Central, for Rahner, to the way in which the acceptance of creatureliness occurs is his identification of God with absolute mystery—"mystery [that] remains a mystery even though it reveals itself."[21] The totality that grounds all the individual things human beings can name is present to them as a question; consequently, human existence itself is experienced as question, or as mystery. The human being is oriented toward absolute mystery as its infinite ground or God, and the stance that one takes toward God is a matter of whether, in freedom, one accepts or rejects this orientation. As Endean puts it, "Rahner's point is that whatever we do and whatever we know are always in some way responsive to a divine initiative which we do not comprehend. All our mental activity is encompassed in a lived emotional stance, some degree of trust or lack of it, some degree of acceptance or rejection of what God has set in motion. Even the rejection of God is grounded in this dark contact between God and the self."[22]

In exercising one's limited freedom in relation to the world, one affirms or rejects one's orientation to God. If one accepts creatureliness, one is obedient to conscience, allowing God to lead one in determining one's choices. To affirm one's orientation to God is to renounce the desire for absolute freedom. It is to accept the uncontrollable in one's own life, trusting one's life to the Holy Mystery that is its ground. "This acceptance takes place in unconditional obedience to conscience, and in the open and trusting acceptance of the uncontrollable in one's own existence in moments of prayer and quiet silence."[23] It is not only, therefore, the case that absolute freedom is an impossibility for human beings; it is precisely the desire for absolute freedom that corrupts authentic human freedom. Authentic *human* freedom lies in giving oneself over the mystery of existence, which communicates itself to human beings as their ground.

The Grounding of Finite Knowledge

Once God and the creator/creature relationship have been properly understood, human knowing comes to be seen in quite a different light from its rationalist and postliberal versions. The knowing subject no longer stands at the center of the epistemological process. The workings of the human mind no longer provide the only justification for truth; rather, God is understood once again as the ground of all human knowing.

In Swinburne and Thiemann, we have found two examples of theologies which are deficient because of their inadequate underlying philosophy of God. We have considered three difficulties that arise for each theology: how to articulate the notion of God's "transcendence"; how to articulate the notion that the infinite can be known by the finite; and how to understand the way in which human knowledge of the finite is grounded. In an attempt to resolve these difficulties, we then turned to Rahner and Schleiermacher with regard to their philosophy of God.

For both Rahner and Schleiermacher, God is known, in human conscious activity as such, as the "other" that grounds the finite. This interpretation proves an effective basis for the resolution of the three main difficulties, as well as the issue of human freedom. Indeed, arguably it is the key to the construction of a sound and comprehensive religious epistemology.

We found that what distinguishes Rahner's approach from that of rationalist and postliberal theologians is his understanding of God as the ground or first cause of existence itself. Schleiermacher effectively bases his theology on an equivalent notion of God as first cause. God is for Rahner the infinite ground, for Schleiermacher the whence, of one's existence. Thus for both theologians, "God" is the name that human beings give to the first cause. On this account, both Rahner and Schleiermacher are able to contextualize their theology within a sound philosophy of God. For Rahner, it is in the context of the openness of the human being to God as its transcendent ground that the doctrine of grace—God's self-gift—is articulated; for Schleiermacher, the doctrine of redemption in Christ is articulated in the context of the impulse of the human being toward God-consciousness. Schleiermacher implicitly and Rahner explicitly include in their understanding of God as first cause an understanding of God as the ground of human knowing. Not only does this common position eliminate the difficulty of articulating God's transcendence; it simultaneously provides the basis for an understanding of how the finite mind may know the infinite, and of how finite knowledge may be grounded. For Rahner and Schleiermacher, not only *is* God "*other*," but God is *known as "other than"* that which is finite, and God is the other that *grounds the "this"*—the finite thing that is known. Thus the question of how the infinite may be known and the question of how the finite may be known, far from requiring different answers in terms of different sorts of knowing, are not even separate questions, since the one question cannot be answered without the other. Knowledge of God, as other than the finite, presupposes knowledge of the finite; knowledge of the finite presupposes knowledge of God as its infinite reference or ground. The one human act of knowing, which occurs in the simultaneous knowledge of the finite and of the infinite, articulates as one of its terms the "otherness" or "transcendence" of God.

Evidence for Belief

It has been possible to discern in the religious epistemologies of Rahner and Schleiermacher a common basic understanding: that God is known, in human conscious activity as such, as the "other" that grounds the finite. How satisfactory is this understanding in terms of meeting the first challenge faced by the Christian apologist in modern times with regard to evidence?

Since the late Middle Ages, the classical arguments for the existence of God have played a significant role in the defense of Christian faith. A priori arguments for the existence of God were fairly quickly called into question, but a posteriori classical arguments continue to occupy a significant place in Christian apologetics. At times Rahner appears dismissive of such arguments, and Schleiermacher is consistently so. Yet a closer analysis reveals that both are involved in a process of refinement rather than an outright repudiation of the classical arguments: Rahner and Schleiermacher do provide evidence for the existence of God. As the ultimate cause/the infinite ground of all finite existence, God self-evidently exists. For both Rahner and Schleiermacher there is an inevitability about positing the existence of God, once the concept to which the word "God" is being applied has been agreed on. Furthermore, the concept of God that each theologian embraces is so similar to the other's that the two are virtually interchangeable. Their evidence is, of course, austere in the extreme. The question is: To what extent does it meet the contemporary demand for evidence? A careful look at how this austere justification relates to the classical arguments will prove useful in making a reply.

For Rahner, God necessarily exists as the condition for human knowing and *human* being; as the infinite horizon of human transcendence, God necessarily exists. As discussed earlier, Rahner sets this necessary existence of God within the broad context of the ontological argument: that which grounds the finite object in the act of knowing cannot be nothingness. It can only be absolute being. By taking the knowing of the single finite object as the context within which God's existence is affirmed, Rahner views his reformulation of the ontological argument as an a posteriori, not an a priori, argument. Insofar as Rahner asserts the necessity for some sort of explanation for the phenomena given in experience, he seems to employ a version of the cosmological argument. His lack of interest in the individual classical arguments, as we have seen, can be explained by the fact that, in his view, all the arguments together can be summed up by the inevitability, in the reflection upon human knowing, of positing the existence of God.

Schleiermacher, as we saw earlier, explicitly dismisses the traditional arguments for the existence of God as irrelevant to piety. His interest is not to prove the existence of God, but rather to examine the workings of the relationship between the human being and God in order to uncover the essence of true religion. According to Schleiermacher, God's existence is self-evident, but even if it were not self-evident, there would be no point in attempting to prove God's existence, since the objective knowledge that would result would be irrelevant to piety. For Schleiermacher, piety takes place in the experience of oneself as absolutely dependent upon another from whom one receives one's existence. Yet despite Schleiermacher's explicit dismissal of the traditional arguments, they are implicit in his work, to the extent that he regards the existence of "God" as the explanation for the feeling of absolute dependence.

The conclusion that we drew earlier was that both Rahner and Schleiermacher regard the traditional arguments for the existence of God as having been in some sense superseded; that whatever form the arguments take, they can be reduced to one argument, drawn from the recognition of the universality of the consciousness of God in the consciousness of oneself as absolutely dependent (Schleiermacher), or drawn from the recognition of the necessity of the transcendental ground as the condition of human knowing (Rahner). Common to the thinking of Rahner and Schleiermacher is the premise that the underlying justification for *all* belief lies in the self-evident existence of God. Their philosophy of God, based on this single claim of evidence, provides the only framework within which the theological truths they profess, even those which are known only by faith, may be justified. The belief that God exists as the whence or the giver of human existence is self-evident, whereas the belief that God gives God's self in grace through the incarnation is a matter of faith—a faith that is grounded in the prior gift of self-conscious existence and in no other way. This is not to say, of course, that the grounding of faith cannot be expressed using different ideas and images, but it does mean that all such expressions have as their only underlying justification the self-evident fact that the totality of human experience derives from another. This austere form of justification underlies all others: it is the claim that there is a place for God as the mysterious other. We have seen that philosophical and theological flaws are immediately apparent once the attempt is made to supply additional or different evidence. That is, these flaws appear when any attempt is made to provide a proof that does not take as its underlying justification the self-evident fact that the totality of human experience derives from another. Or, in other words, the flaws appear when any evidence is put forward that is not based on a sound philosophy of God as ultimate or first cause.

Thiemann's attitude toward the justification of belief, as we found, is ambiguous. He thinks that the doctrine of revelation must be defended in a rational manner. Yet in the Lutheran/Barthian tradition, Thiemann considers that there is no "natural" knowledge of God—none that does not result from direct revelation. He sees no place for arguments for the existence of God. If, however, the essence of the arguments is the self-evident existence of God as first cause, then to ignore the arguments is to fail to understand God as first cause. It amounts to failing to consider ultimate questions about human experience itself or existence itself. Yet without these considerations, it is impossible to articulate a sound theology.

In Swinburne's philosophical theology, we found that not too few but rather too many concessions had been made to the demand for evidence; more fundamentally, Swinburne's evidence fails because it has been removed from the context of a sound philosophy of God. This is the case with regard both to his defense of the coherence of theism and to his defense of the rationality of Christian belief. Thomas Aquinas warned that the reality of God can only be articulated in terms of what God is not. Swinburne ignores this warning and attempts to give evidence for God's substantive content.

Rahner and Schleiermacher, on the other hand, make no attempt to give evidence for God's substantive content. Schleiermacher, as we have seen, says nothing about the "content" of God, but merely that God—whatever that might be—is in some sense given to the human being in piety. Consequent upon this understanding, he sets out certain conditions regarding what *may not* be said of God. He offers no substantive explanation of God, but rather a series of conditions—negative rules—which must be satisfied if more is to be said. Rahner, likewise, says nothing in a strictly philosophical context about the "content" of the word "God," which as a word merely functions as a proper name. The notion that God is a self-giving God derives not from evidence but from faith.

If one considers the question of what constitutes sufficient evidence for the existence of God, therefore, one finds that the only evidence possible is some version of the self-evident notion of God as first cause of existence itself. Any exposition which either falls short of this notion, or attempts to fill out the notion without reference to God's self-gift in revelation, cannot uphold the idea of God's transcendence.

The Key

This book began with two challenges to Christian faith: the need for evidence to support anything proposed for faith, and the need to recognize that human experience is mediated. It was necessary to take into account, on the one hand, certain requirements of Christianity (the need to articulate God's "transcendence," that it must be possible for the finite to know the infinite); and on the other hand, certain anthropological requirements (the need for a sound version of human knowing, and the less strictly epistemological need for a sound version of human freedom). It is significant to note that in attending to the requirements of Christianity (that God is transcendent, and that it must be possible for the finite mind to know God), the anthropological requirement (that human knowing must be grounded) has also been met.

The fundamental argument of this book is that there can be no sound religious epistemology that is not based on the premodern notion of God as first cause of existence itself; it is precisely the failure to recognize God as first cause, in the sense explained here, that has confounded the attempts of numerous rationalist and postliberal theologians alike to find solutions to the problems that beset religious epistemology.

From this understanding of God as first cause of existence itself, it has been possible to arrive at a definition of human freedom that reaches beyond the strictly epistemological to the more broadly anthropological. The fact that the human being knows itself to have an "other" as its ground, that is to say, the very creatureliness of the human being, means that none of its characteristics can be defined outside the context of its relationship to its creator/God. The essential characteristic of the human being is that it is conscious that it derives its being from, and continues to owe its identity to, an "other," which it calls "God." A parallel finding, therefore, in the search for a sound Christian apologetic is that there can be no separation between philosophical theology and anthropology, since to engage in one is to engage in the other.

With regard to the demand for evidence, this study concludes that the only evidence that can be brought in defense of the rationality of Christian belief is that a proper analysis of the human being necessarily posits God as its transcendental ground. Following Rahner and Schleiermacher, we conclude that this one piece of evidence provides the only framework within which theological truths that are professed may be justified. All the traditional arguments for God's existence can be reduced to this one argument, and it is only within the context of this one argument that God's gracious self-gift—the essence of Christian faith—may be soundly articulated.

Since all human experience and therefore knowledge is mediated by the finite, it is clear that it must be in our involvement with the concrete world that the experience of God occurs. Rahner shows that it is precisely in the historical reaching out beyond the finite thing in order to know it that the human being knows God. The key, therefore, to a sound religious epistemology is this: that God is known in human conscious activity as such as the "other" that grounds the finite. This understanding is common to the philosophical theologies of both Rahner and Schleiermacher. Their approach to questions of God, the self, and human knowledge overcomes significant difficulties besetting much modern theology.

Finally, one of the questions that has been at issue in this work has been how to determine the appropriate relationship between philosophy and theology. When the role played by philosophy in a given theological outlook has been considered inappropriate, the theology has often been described as "foundationalist." Yet once this description has been applied, it has seemed to follow that no philosophical grounding at all is possible without risking the foundationalist label. And yet with no philosophical grounding at all, the theological enterprise itself is impossible. What matters for authentic theology is that the distinction is carefully drawn between the necessary role that philosophy plays in theological interpretation, and the equally necessary principle that philosophical thinking does not presume to determine the content of revelation that is the subject matter of the theological undertaking.

NOTES

Chapter 1. **Swinburne and Rationalism**

1. Richard Swinburne, *The Coherence of Theism* (Oxford: Clarendon Press, 1977; reprint, 1993).
2. Richard Swinburne, *The Existence of God* (Oxford: Clarendon Press, 1979; revised edition, 1991). I use the 1991 revised edition.
3. Richard Swinburne, *Faith and Reason* (Oxford: Clarendon Press, 1981; revised edition, 2005). I use the 2005 revised edition.
4. Swinburne, *The Coherence of Theism*, 1.
5. Swinburne, *Faith and Reason*, 198.
6. A. J. Ayer compares the meaning of religious assertions with the meaning of the sentence "There is a 'drogulus' over there," where a "drogulus" cannot be described or touched, has no physical effects, and there is no way of telling that it is there. Ayer considers that, like the sentence about the "drogulus," religious assertions are nonsense. See A. J. Ayer, "Logical Positivism—A Debate," in *A Modern Introduction to Philosophy*, ed. P. Edwards and A. Pap, rev. ed. (New York: The Free Press, 1965), 747.
7. Richard Swinburne, "Intellectual Autobiography," in *Reason and the Christian Religion: Essays in Honour of Richard Swinburne*, ed. Alan G. Padgett (Oxford: Clarendon Press, 1994), 3.
8. Swinburne, *The Coherence of Theism*, 81.
9. Ibid., 77.
10. Ibid., 81.
11. Swinburne, "Intellectual Autobiography," 4.
12. Ibid., 5.
13. J. Neuner and J. Dupuis, eds., *The Christian Faith in the Doctrinal Documents of the Catholic Church* (London: Collins Liturgical Publications, 1983), 109.

14. See Thomas Aquinas, *Summa contra Gentiles,* vol. 1, trans. A.C. Pegis (New York: Image Books, 1955).

15. Thomas Aquinas, *Summa Theologiae* 1a, 13, 5. Vol. 3, ed. Herbert McCabe (London: Blackfriars, 1964).

16. Aquinas, *Summa Theologiae* 1a, 13, 5.

17. Richard Dawkins, *The Blind Watchmaker* (Harlow, U.K.: Longman Scientific and Technical, 1986); Stephen Hawking, *A Brief History of Time* (London: Bantam Press, 1988).

18. Richard Swinburne, *Is There a God?* (Oxford: Oxford University Press, 1996), 1–2.

19. Swinburne, "Intellectual Autobiography," 8.

20. Swinburne, *Is There a God?*, 2.

21. Ibid., 20.

22. Ibid., 38.

23. Ibid., 48.

24. Swinburne, "Intellectual Autobiography," 5.

25. Ibid., 7–8.

26. Swinburne, *Is There a God?*, 68.

27. Ibid., 86–90.

28. Preface to the *Proslogion,* quoted in *Anselm of Canterbury: The Major Works,* ed. Brian Davies and G.R. Evans (Oxford: Oxford University Press, 1998), 83.

29. Swinburne, *The Existence of God,* 9.

30. Ibid., 9.

31. Ibid., 244.

32. Ibid., 9.

33. Ibid., 7–8.

34. Ibid., 244.

35. Ibid., 247.

36. Ibid., 246.

37. Ibid., 247.

38. Ibid., 275.

39. C.B. Martin, "A Religious Way of Knowing," in *New Essays in Philosophical Theology,* ed. A. Flew and A. MacIntyre (London: SCM Press, 1955), 76–95.

40. C. Taliaferro, *Contemporary Philosophy of Religion* (Oxford: Blackwell, 1998), 265.

41. See Richard Gale, *On the Nature and Existence of God* (Cambridge: Cambridge University Press, 1991), 298–99.

42. Swinburne, *The Existence of God,* 274.

43. Ibid., 289.

44. Ibid., 291.

45. Ibid., 244.
46. Otto Muck, "Assumptions of a Classical Philosophy of God," *Milltown Studies* 33 (1994): 37–50.
47. See Thomas Aquinas, *Summa Theologiae* 1a, 2, 1. Vol. 2, ed. T. McDermott (London: Blackfriars, 1964).
48. Muck, "Assumptions of a Classical Philosophy of God," 38.
49. See Thomas Aquinas, *Summa Theologiae* 1a, 2, 3. Vol. 2, ed. McDermott.
50. Muck, "Assumptions of a Classical Philosophy of God," 38–39.
51. Ibid., 41.
52. Swinburne, *Faith and Reason*, 137.
53. Ibid.
54. Ibid., 4.
55. Ibid., 151.
56. Ibid., 151–52.
57. Ibid., 228.
58. Ibid., 228–30.
59. Ibid., 217.
60. Ibid., 146.
61. Ibid., 167. In the first (1981) edition Swinburne suggests that the "first good purpose for a man to pursue a religious way . . . is to obtain salvation for oneself (130). The second is "to secure salvation for others," and the third is "to render due worship and obedience to God" (138).
62. Ibid., 188–89.
63. Ibid., 189 n. 38.
64. "Dogmatic Constitution *Dei Filius* on the Catholic Faith," 1870, in J. Neuner and J. Dupuis, *The Christian Faith*, 41.

Chapter 2. **Postliberalism and Lindbeck**

1. Justin argues that on some points Christians teach the same things as the poets and philosophers of the Gnostics, but "on other points [we] are fuller and more divine in our teaching" (Justin, *The First Apology of Justin* [Kila, Mont.: Kessinger Publishing, 2004], chap. 20).
2. For further information on postliberal theology, see William C. Placher, "Postliberal Theology," in *The Modern Theologians: An Introduction to Christian Theology in the Twentieth Century*, ed. David F. Ford, rev. ed. (Oxford: Blackwell, 1997), 343–56.
3. George A. Lindbeck, *The Nature of Doctrine: Religion and Theology in a Postliberal Age* (London: SPCK; Philadelphia: Westminster Press, 1984).
4. Ronald F. Thiemann, *Revelation and Theology: The Gospel as Narrated Promise* (Notre Dame, Ind.: University of Notre Dame Press, 1985).

5. While Lindbeck's own involvement has been chiefly in Roman Catholic/Lutheran dialogue (see *The Nature of Doctrine*, 26 n. 1), and while the epistemologies he challenges belong to the Western tradition, Lindbeck nonetheless believes that his "cultural-linguistic" approach has implications for interreligious dialogue (see chap. 3 in particular). In his constructive work he draws freely on ideas from both Orthodox Christianity (e.g., 102–3) and non-Christian religions (e.g., 100–101).

6. What I have called a conservative propositional model of revelation, Lindbeck labels a propositionalist or cognitivist approach. He regards this as a preliberal approach, and includes in it traditional orthodoxies such as that of Thomas Aquinas. What I have called a liberal experiential model, Lindbeck labels an experiential-expressivist or symbolic approach. He regards this as a liberal approach, influenced by Kant, and he attributes this approach to Friedrich Schleiermacher, Rudolf Otto, Rudolf Bultmann, and Paul Tillich. Further, Lindbeck refers to two sorts of propositionalists: old-fashioned and modern. Also he places some thinkers under both a modern propositionalist and an experiential-expressivist heading: e.g., Karl Rahner and Bernard Lonergan.

7. Lindbeck, *The Nature of Doctrine*, 17–18.

8. Ibid., 33.

9. Swinburne, *Faith and Reason*, 119.

10. Lindbeck, *The Nature of Doctrine*, 16.

11. Ibid., 69.

12. Ibid., 47, quotes from Bernard Lonergan, *Insight: A Study of Human Understanding* (London: Harper and Row, 1978), 399.

13. Lindbeck, *The Nature of Doctrine*, 47.

14. Ibid., 48.

15. Ibid., 64.

16. Ibid., 63.

17. Ibid., 66.

18. Ibid., 64.

19. Ibid., 66.

20. Ibid., 51.

21. Austin is at some pains to stress that he simply means what he says. See J. L. Austin, "Performative Utterances," in *Philosophical Papers*, ed. J. O. Urmson and G. J. Warnock, 2d ed. (Oxford: Clarendon Press, 1970), 233.

22. Ibid., 235.

23. Lindbeck, *The Nature of Doctrine*, 65. Austin states specifically regarding marriage: "But the one thing we must not suppose is that what is needed in addition to the saying of the words in such cases is the performance of some internal spiritual act, of which the words then are to be the report" ("Perfor-

mative Utterances," in *Philosophical Papers*, 236). Lindbeck does not suggest that the words "report" the act, but rather suggests that the words produce a correspondence. The words are both performative and propositional at the same time.

24. Lindbeck, *The Nature of Doctrine*, 65.
25. Ibid., 66.
26. Ibid., 66–67. Lindbeck quotes from *Summa Theologiae* 1a, 13, 3. See *Summa Theologiae*, vol. 3, ed. Herbert McCabe; see also *Summa contra Gentiles* 1, 30, in *Summa contra Gentiles*, vol. 1, trans. A. C. Pegis.
27. Lindbeck, *The Nature of Doctrine*, 69.
28. Ibid., 20–21.
29. Ibid., 30.
30. Ibid., 23.
31. Ibid., 22.
32. Ibid., 23.
33. Bernard Lonergan, *Method in Theology* (London: Darton, Longman and Todd, 1972).
34. Lindbeck, *The Nature of Doctrine*, 31–32.
35. Ibid., 32; quotes from Bernard Lonergan, *Philosophy of God and Theology* (London: Darton, Longman and Todd, 1973), 50.
36. Lindbeck, *The Nature of Doctrine*, 32; quotes from Lonergan, *Method in Theology*, 108.
37. Lonergan, *Method in Theology*, 109, summarizes Friedrich Heiler's "The History of Religion as a Preparation for the Cooperation of Religions," in *The History of Religions*, ed. M. Eliade, and J. Kitagawa (Chicago: University of Chicago Press, 1959), 142–53.
38. Lindbeck, *The Nature of Doctrine*, 23; Lindbeck paraphrases a remark of Santayana, cited without exact reference by C. Geertz, "Religion as a Cultural System," in his *The Interpretation of Cultures: Selected Essays* (New York: Basic Books, 1973), 87.
39. Lindbeck, *The Nature of Doctrine*, 32, my emphasis.
40. Ibid., 32.

Chapter 3. **The Anti-foundationalism of Thiemann**

1. Thiemann, *Revelation and Theology*, 2.
2. Ibid., 157 n. 2, quoting from Werner Elert, *Der christliche Glaube* (Hamburg: Furche Verlag, 1956), 134–35. Thiemann also refers here to Gustaf Wingren, *Theology in Conflict* (Philadelphia: Muhlenberg, 1958), 23–44 and 108–28.

3. Thiemann, *Revelation and Theology*, 1, quoting from Stanley Hauerwas, *A Community of Character* (Notre Dame, Ind.: University of Notre Dame Press, 1981), 57.

4. Thiemann, *Revelation and Theology*, 3.

5. Ibid., 3.

6. Ibid., 4.

7. Ibid., 7.

8. Barth immediately springs to mind as an exception, but Thiemann makes no specific mention of Barth at this point (see Thiemann, *Revelation and Theology*, 1). Thiemann may intend to include Barth here, since he equates a defense of the doctrine of revelation with a defense of God's prevenience; and as I have indicated, he regards Luther and Barth as theologians who classically uphold the notion of God's prevenience.

9. Thiemann, *Revelation and Theology*, 16–17.

10. Ibid., 24–31.

11. Ibid., 26.

12. Ibid., 27, quoting from Schleiermacher, *The Christian Faith* (New York: Harper and Row, 1963), 50.

13. Thiemann, *Revelation and Theology*, 28–29.

14. Ibid., 48.

15. Ibid., 40, quoting from Richard Rorty, *Philosophy and the Mirror of Nature* (Princeton: Princeton University Press, 1979), 157.

16. Thiemann, *Revelation and Theology*, 32.

17. Ibid., 32.

18. Ibid., 33.

19. Thomas Torrance, *Theological Science* (Oxford: Oxford University Press, 1969), 89.

20. Thiemann, *Revelation and Theology*, 39, quoting from Torrance, *Theological Science*, 129–31. Thiemann in fact misquotes Torrance and refers to "an intuitive apprehension of the whole pattern of *faith*."

21. Thiemann, *Revelation and Theology*, 42–43.

22. Ibid., 18, quoting from John Locke, *An Essay Concerning Human Understanding*, vol. 2 (New York: Dover, 1959), 438.

23. Locke, *Essay*, 412.

24. Thiemann, *Revelation and Theology*, 18.

25. Locke, *Essay*, 416.

26. Thiemann, *Revelation and Theology*, 17.

27. Ibid., 165 n. 40.

28. Ibid., 40. Thiemann's comment that Torrance's Kierkegaardian starting point is nonfoundational is interesting in itself, revealing as it does Thiemann's own leanings. Presumably he refers to the fact that Torrance accepts the absolute contrast between faith and reason.

29. Ibid., 40, referring to Torrance, *Theological Science*, 141–61.
30. Karl Rahner, *Hearer of the Word*, trans. Joseph Donceel (New York: Continuum, 1994), 18–19.
31. Thiemann, *Revelation and Theology*, 30.
32. Ibid., 163 n. 21.
33. Karl Rahner, *Spirit in the World*, trans. William V. Dych (London: Sheed and Ward, 1968), 25–38.
34. Thiemann, *Revelation and Theology*, 48–49.
35. Ibid., 40.
36. Ibid., 151.
37. Ibid., 47–48.
38. Ibid., 40.
39. Ibid., 167 n. 1.
40. Ibid., 153.
41. Ibid., 153–54.
42. Ibid., 153.
43. Ibid., 47.
44. Ibid., 153.
45. Ibid., 49.
46. Ibid., 57, quoting from David Kelsey, *Uses of Scripture in Recent Theology* (Philadelphia: Fortress Press, 1975), 89.
47. Thiemann, *Revelation and Theology*, 57, quoting from Kelsey, *Uses of Scripture*, 102.
48. Thiemann, *Revelation and Theology*, 58, quoting from Kelsey, *Uses of Scripture*, 159.
49. This type of "narrative theology" originates with the early works of Hans Frei, in which he claimed that reading the Bible as a realistic narrative was more faithful to the meaning of these texts than alternatives. In later work Frei talks of the "literal reading" of biblical narrative. (See William C. Placher, "Postliberal Theology," in *The Modern Theologians: An Introduction to Christian Theology in the Twentieth Century*, ed. David Ford, rev. ed. (Oxford: Blackwell, 1997), 351. Wood also talks of the "literal sense" of the biblical text.
50. Thiemann, *Revelation and Theology*, 65, quoting from Charles Wood, *The Formation of Christian Understanding: An Essay in Theological Hermeneutics* (Philadelphia: Westminster Press, 1981), 100–101.
51. Thiemann, *Revelation and Theology*, 56, quoting from Wood, *The Formation of Christian Understanding*, 22. It is not my intention here to criticize in any detailed way the functional view put forward by Wood. However, it is worth noting that the sentence "'The text means' is always elliptical" is itself an elliptical sentence—yet not on that account without a meaning which can be understood.
52. Thiemann, *Revelation and Theology*, 56.

53. Ibid., 58, quoting from Kelsey, *Uses of Scripture*, 97–98.
54. Thiemann, *Revelation and Theology*, 58–59, quoting from Kelsey, *Uses of Scripture*, 109.
55. Thiemann, *Revelation and Theology*, 69.
56. Ibid., 69–70.
57. Ibid., 70.
58. Ibid., 82.
59. Ibid., 153.
60. Ibid., 72.
61. See W. L. Reese, *Dictionary of Philosophy and Religion* (Atlantic Highlands, N.J.: Humanities Press, 1980), 128.
62. Thiemann, *Revelation and Theology*, 178 n. 4.
63. Ibid., 72.
64. Ibid., 75.
65. Ibid., 79. Thiemann refers to James Barr, *The Bible in the Modern World* (New York: Harper and Row, 1973), 121.
66. Thiemann, *Revelation and Theology*, 80.
67. Ibid., 81–82.
68. Wolfhart Pannenberg, *Jesus—God and Man*, trans. Lewis L. Wilkins and Duane A. Priebe (London: SCM Press, 1968), 107.
69. Thiemann, *Revelation and Theology*, 93.
70. Ibid., 95.
71. Ibid., 94.
72. Ibid., 99–100, referring to J.L. Austin, "Performative Utterances," in *Philosophical Papers*, 238. Austin develops his "speech-act theory" at length in *How to Do Things with Words* (Cambridge, Mass.: Harvard University Press, 1962).
73. Thiemann, *Revelation and Theology*, 99.
74. Ibid., 100–101.
75. Ibid., 143.
76. Ibid., 145.
77. Ibid., 146.
78. Ibid., 147.
79. Ibid., 144.
80. Ibid., 144–45. The emphasis is mine.
81. Ibid., 147.

Chapter 4. **Schleiermacher and Absolute Dependence**

1. Friedrich Schleiermacher, *On Religion: Speeches to Its Cultured Despisers*, trans. and ed. Richard Crouter (Cambridge: Cambridge University Press, 1988),

henceforth referred to as *Speeches*. German edition, *Über die Religion: Reden an die Gebildeten unter ihren Verächtern* (Stuttgart: Reclam, 1969).

2. Schleiermacher considered his revisions to *Über die Religion* of 1806 and 1821 to be more stylistic than substantive. Crouter, "A Note on Editions," in *Speeches*, xliv, comments that the revisions were intended to play down Schleiermacher's apparent heterodoxy, to give the rhetoric of the text a more "scientific" form, and to address changing circumstances affecting Protestantism in Berlin.

3. Friedrich Schleiermacher, *The Christian Faith*, trans. and ed. H. R. Mackintosh and J. S. Stewart (2 vols., New York: Harper and Row, 1963; 1 vol., Edinburgh: T & T Clark, 1999). My citations are from the T & T Clark 1999 edition. German edition, *Der christliche Glaube*, rev. ed. (1830/1831), ed. Martin Redeker (Berlin and New York: Walter de Gruyter, 1999).

4. Friedrich Schleiermacher, *Der christliche Glaube*, 1st ed. (1821/1822), 2 vols., ed. Hermann Peiter (Berlin and New York: Walter de Gruyter, 1984).

5. See Richard Niebuhr, *Schleiermacher on Christ and Religion* (London: SCM Press, 1965), 6, and B. A. Gerrish, *A Prince of the Church: Schleiermacher and the Beginnings of Modern Theology* (London: SCM Press, 1984), 6.

6. In the English-speaking world, perhaps the leading exponent of Schleiermacher's work, and a favorable commentator, is B. A. Gerrish. See in particular his *A Prince of the Church*.

7. Emil Brunner, *Die Mystik und das Wort* (Tübingen: J. C. B. Mohr, 1924).

8. Brunner, for example, contrasts his own definition of faith with Schleiermacher's "feeling of absolute dependence," saying, "Faith is the attitude of those who simply receive. It is the very opposite of all self-knowledge, self-assurance, or self-possession. A man only really believes where everything depends upon his receptivity, where he is utterly dependent and helpless. By this I mean something quite different from the 'feeling of absolute dependence' advocated by Schleiermacher. This phrase sounds far more Christian than it really is. It means nothing more than the consciousness of causal determination; it is not the admission of a personal relationship." Emil Brunner, *The Mediator* (London and Redhill: Lutterworth Press, 1934), 299. Referring to Karl Barth's *Die Theologie und die Kirche* (Zurich, 1928), Richard Niebuhr comments, "Barth . . . was not above treating (Schleiermacher's) thinking in a lofty fashion, indiscriminately mixing together materials gathered from a period covering thirty years or more of Schleiermacher's authorship and preaching, and offering as his distillate of this brew the doctrine: peace is truth" (*Schleiermacher on Christ and Religion*, 7).

9. Schleiermacher, *Speeches*, 19–20.

10. Ibid., 20.

11. Schleiermacher, *The Christian Faith*, 82–83.

12. Ibid., 83.

13. According to Hermann Fischer, "Schleiermacher's *The Christian Faith* may be taken to represent the work of classical evangelical systematic theology in modern times. Its significance lies in the fact that Schleiermacher undertakes a complete revision of traditional dogmatics in accordance with Kant's critique of knowledge, and Kant's insight with regard to transcendental philosophy." Hermann Fischer, *Friedrich Schleiermacher* (Munich: Verlag C. H. Beck, 2001), 97–98 (my translation).

14. Schleiermacher, *The Christian Faith*, 16.
15. Ibid., 244.
16. Ibid., 238.
17. Ibid., 244.
18. Ibid.
19. Ibid., 54–55.
20. Ibid., 52.
21. Ibid., 57–58.
22. Ibid., 56.
23. Ibid., 387.
24. Thiemann, *Revelation and Theology*, 27.
25. Ibid., 29.
26. Schleiermacher, *Speeches*, 22.
27. Ibid., 22.
28. Ibid., 23.
29. Keith W. Clements talks of a "relative indifference to religion among the educated classes, who were casually grateful to the philosophers for conveniently adducing intellectual grounds for their scepticism." Clements, *Friedrich Schleiermacher: Pioneer of Modern Theology* (London: Collins, 1987), 11.
30. Schleiermacher, *Speeches*, 23–24.
31. Ibid.
32. *The Christian Faith*, 26. Significantly, Schleiermacher insists that the religious is not subject to external standards of verification.
33. Crouter, in *Speeches*, 26. Crouter refers to Fichte, *Sämtliche Werke* 1 (Berlin, 1845), 91ff.
34. Schleiermacher, *Speeches*, 26; for German see *Über die Religion*, 40–41.
35. Crouter, in *Speeches*, 26 n. 11.
36. Schleiermacher, *Speeches*, 31 n. 16.
37. Hegel first lectured on philosophy of religion in 1821, and repeated the series with revisions in 1824, 1827, and 1831. Hegel did not publish his lectures, but they became available from notes taken down by his students. See P. C. Hodgson's "Editorial Introduction," in G. W. F. Hegel, *Lectures on the Philosophy of Religion*, vol. 1, ed. P. C. Hodgson (Berkeley: University of California Press, 1984), 2–4.

38. For Hegel's foreword, see H. F. W. Hinrichs, *Die Religion im inneren Verhältnisse zur Wissenschaft* (Heidelberg, 1822), i–xxviii, especially xviii–xix. For the original German text of 1822, see "Hegels *Hinrichs-Vorwort*: Kritische Ausgabe," which appears as an appendix to *Hegel, Hinrichs, and Schleiermacher on Feeling and Reason in Religion: The Texts of Their 1821–1822 Debate*, trans. and ed. E. Luft (New York: Edwin Mellen Press, 1987), 490–520; for an English translation, see 245–68 in the same volume.

39. Hodgson, "Editorial Introduction" to Hegel, *Lectures on the Philosophy of Religion*, 11.

40. Hegel, *Lectures on the Philosophy of Religion*, 136.

41. Michael J. Buckley, *At the Origins of Modern Atheism* (New Haven: Yale University Press, 1987), 330–32.

42. Ibid., 332.

43. For an argument that Feuerbach does not represent the outcome, much less the fulfillment, of Schleiermacher, see R. Williams, "Schleiermacher and Feuerbach on the Intentionality of Religious Consciousness," *The Journal of Religion* 53 (1973): 424–55. In support of the view that Feuerbach knowingly misrepresents Schleiermacher, see John Macquarrie, *Jesus Christ in Modern Thought* (London: SCM Press, 1990), 194. For the view that Feuerbach rejects Hegel's criticism of Schleiermacher and attempts to align Schleiermacher's thinking to his own, see E. Brito, *La Pneumatologie de Schleiermacher* (Louvain: Louvain University Press, 1994), 425–26. For the view that the influence of Schleiermacher on Feuerbach is open to question, see *Hegel, Hinrichs, and Schleiermacher on Feeling and Reason in Religion*, ed. Luft, 285 n. 7.

44. Ludwig Feuerbach, *Lectures on the Essence of Religion* (New York: Harper and Row, 1967), 25. Hegel, making a distinction between what an animal "feels" and what a human being "knows," comments: "It is the superiority of what is living to feel its limit; and still more it is the superiority of what is spiritual to *know* its limit. The animal feels its limit—it is fearful, hungry, thirsty, and so forth. There is a breach in its feeling of self-reliance; there is a negation in it, and the feeling of this negation is present. The animal feels pain and is afraid; it takes fright when it is hunted and comes to a wall; there it feels its limit. If we say that religion rests on this feeling of dependence, then animals would have to have religion too, for they feel this dependence. The limit, however, only exists for me inasmuch as I pass beyond it; in feeling, in being conscious of the limit, the passing beyond it is implied." Hegel, "The Lectures of 1824," *Lectures on the Philosophy of Religion*, 279–80.

45. Ludwig Feuerbach, *Sämtliche Werke*, vol. 7, *Erläuterungen und Ergänzungen zum Wesen des Christenthums* (Stuttgart–Bad Cannstadt: Günther Holzboog, 1960), 226, my translation.

46. Schleiermacher, *Speeches*, 3–4.

47. Translation from Julia A. Lamm, *The Living God: Schleiermacher's Theological Appropriation of Spinoza* (University Park: Pennsylvania State University, 1996), 110–11. German, *Der christliche Glaube* (1821/1822), vol. 1, 31.

48. Lamm considers that although Schleiermacher's revisions suggest that he was concerned to rebut the charge of subjective idealism, he was in fact primarily concerned to distinguish his own position from an unacceptable pantheism.

49. Lamm, *The Living God*, 111.

50. Schleiermacher, *The Christian Faith*, 12; German, *Der christliche Glaube* (1830/1831), 23.

51. Thiemann, *Revelation and Theology*, 29.

52. Schleiermacher, *The Christian Faith*, 16.

53. Ibid., 16.

54. Ibid., 18.

55. Ibid., 16.

56. Lamm, *The Living God*, 193, referring to Schleiermacher, *The Christian Faith*, 18.

57. Schleiermacher, *The Christian Faith*, 18.

58. Ibid., 133–34.

59. Ibid., 136.

60. Thiemann, *Revelation and Theology*, 27–28.

61. Schleiermacher, *The Christian Faith*, 12.

62. Ibid., 722.

63. Ibid., 720–22. Schleiermacher gives the biblical references only. Quotations are from the Revised Standard Version, Catholic edition, 1966.

64. Ibid., 136–37.

65. Ibid., 17–18.

66. Nicholas Lash, *Easter in Ordinary* (London: SCM Press, 1988), 127.

Chapter 5. **Rahner's "God"**

1. Karl Rahner, *Spirit in the World*, trans. William V. Dych (London: Sheed and Ward, 1968). Translation of the German edition *Geist in Welt: Zur Metaphysik der endlichen Erkenntnis bei Thomas von Aquin* (Innsbruck: Rauch, 1939). Also available as *Geist in Welt*, in Karl Rahner, *Sämtliche Werke*, Band 2 (Solothurn and Düsseldorf: Benziger; Freiburg: Herder, 1996). My citations from *Geist in Welt* are from *Sämtliche Werke*.

2. *Hörer des Wortes* (*Hearer of the Word*), which developed from Rahner's lectures at a summer school in Salzburg in 1937, was first published in 1941. A second edition, revised by Johannes Baptist Metz, 1963, included much of Metz's own thought. This was translated into English by Michael Richards as

Hearers of the Word (New York: Herder & Herder, 1969). The original German text of 1941 was subsequently translated by Joseph Donceel, edited by Andrew Tallon (New York: Continuum, 1994). I use the Donceel translation; for the German I cite the original 1941 edition and its page numbers as reprinted in Karl Rahner, *Sämtliche Werke*, Band 4 (Solothurn and Düsseldorf: Benziger, and Freiburg: Herder, 1997).

3. Karl Rahner, *Foundations of Christian Faith: An Introduction to the Idea of Christianity*, trans. William V. Dych (New York: Crossroad, 1998). English translation of *Grundkurs des Glaubens: Einführung in den Begriff des Christentums* (Freiburg: Herder, 1984).

4. This argument is put forward most notably by Karen Kilby, *Karl Rahner: Theology and Philosophy* (London and New York: Routledge, 2004).

5. Rahner, *Foundations*, 84–85.

6. Ibid., 55.

7. This definition of *species intelligibilis* is taken from George Vass, *A Theologian in Search of a Philosophy: Understanding Karl Rahner*, vol. 1 (London: Sheed and Ward, 1985), 31.

8. Rahner writes, "This knowledge is supposed to be based on (*convertere*) things (*phantasmata*), and yet as universal and necessary knowledge is supposed to judge these things" [*Sie selbst soll auf den Dingen (phantasmata) beruhen (convertere) und soll doch als allgemeine und notwendige Erkenntis diese Dinge beurteilen*]. *Spirit in the World*, 21; *Geist in Welt*, 28.

9. Rahner, *Spirit in the World*, 27.

10. *Summa Theologiae* 1, q. 84, a. 7. See Thomas Aquinas, *Summa Theologiae*, vol. 12, trans. P. T. Durbin (London: Blackfriars, 1968).

11. Karl Rahner, *Hearer of the Word*, 2–3.

12. Fergus Kerr, *Theology after Wittgenstein*, rev. ed. (London: SPCK, 1997), 14. (First edition, Basil Blackwell, 1986; the criticism appears in both editions.)

13. According to Kerr's later thinking, "Rahner had no doubt about the impossibility of incorporating the ideal of any wordless self into Christian theology." But Rahner knew that theology could not avoid the turn to subject, because the turn to subject is also most profoundly Christian. It does not reduce the human being to "one factor in a cosmos of things" subservient to a conceptual system of how things are. Instead it posits the human being as "the subject on whose freedom as subject hangs the fate of the whole cosmos." In Kerr's view it is this latter conception that allows the history of God's dispensation of grace to have cosmological significance. Fergus Kerr, *Immortal Longings: Versions of Transcending Humanity* (London: SPCK, 1997), 175–76.

14. Rahner, *Foundations*, 17–18.

15. Kerr, *Theology after Wittgenstein* (1997), 10.

16. In his later work Wittgenstein rejects the notion of a private language and argues that language cannot be logically available only to one speaker. He

thus rejects the notion of the Cartesian subject, who is able to discourse alone about his private inner experience. Wittgenstein argues that language can only be acquired in a public setting. Language requires some agreement, which he calls a "form of life," concerning the use of words. Without "use" there can be no language. Similarly, unobservable mental states cannot come about except in a public setting. See *Philosophy 1: A Guide through the Subject*, ed. A. C. Grayling (New York: Oxford University Press, 1995), 56.

17. Rahner, *Foundations*, 21.
18. Ibid., 46.
19. Philip Endean, *Karl Rahner and Ignatian Spirituality* (Oxford: Oxford University Press, 2001), 166.
20. Ibid., 152–53.
21. Ibid., 52.
22. Rahner, *Foundations*, 15–16.
23. Ibid., 47.
24. Ibid., 48–49.
25. Ibid., 52.
26. Ibid.
27. Ibid., 46.
28. Rahner, *Hearer of the Word*, 8.
29. Ibid., 9.
30. See Rahner, ch. 6, "Jesus Christ," in *Foundations*.
31. Karl Rahner, "The Hermeneutics of Eschatological Assertions," in *Theological Investigations*, vol. 4 (London: Darton, Longman & Todd, 1966), 330.
32. Ibid., 331.
33. Rahner, *Foundations*, 59.
34. Rahner, *Spirit in the World*, 53–54.
35. Ibid., 393.
36. Rahner, *Foundations*, 21.
37. Ibid., 34–35; *Grundkurs des Glaubens*, 45.
38. Rahner, *Hearer of the Word*, 47; *Hörer des Wortes* (1941), 76.
39. Following the distinction made in Scholastic theology between the material and the formal object, Rahner uses *Gegenstand* to refer to the material object of knowledge, while *Objekt* refers to the formal object of knowledge. The formal object of Scholastic theology was identified with the specific viewpoint that the knower takes toward the material object. Philip Endean gives the following example of the type of distinction that would be made according to the Scholastic model: For a psychologist the material object of study would be the human person, while the formal object would be "those aspects of the human on which, abstracting from others, psychology focuses." The formal object includes an orientation in the knowing subject which enables the subject to know the formal object. However, Rahner's transcendental philosophy

goes further than this, applying the term "formal object" to the knower. The formal object includes an orientation in the knowing subject which enables the subject to know the formal object (Endean, *Karl Rahner and Ignatian Spirituality*, 36–38). This orientation toward knowledge of God as the infinite horizon of human transcendence is what Rahner terms the "supernatural existential" (*Foundations*, 126–28).

40. Rahner, *Hörer des Wortes* (1941), 79, my translation. The word *worauf*, translated by Donceel as "whither" ("whither does human anticipating knowing transcend the single object which it grasps"? *Hearer of the Word*, 49), is better translated by "on what basis," which excludes the idea of movement toward a goal. Philip Endean discusses the meaning of *auf* in *Woraufhin*—the sustaining basis of the *Vorgriff* (*Karl Rahner and Ignatian Spirituality*, 155–56, n. 6).

41. Rahner, *Hearer of the Word*, 49.
42. Ibid., 51.
43. Rahner, *Hearer of the Word*, 26.
44. Rahner, *Foundations*, 70.
45. Kilby, *Karl Rahner*, 10.
46. Ibid.
47. Ibid., 10 and passim.
48. Ibid., 10.
49. The same applies to natural philosophy or science. Some basic scientific knowledge is a precondition for any understanding of what revelation teaches about God and the world. Without some basic knowledge of the way in which living things grow and die, without some basic knowledge of the process of procreation and the physical interrelatedness of human beings, without some basic concept of the structure of the world, the Christian Gospel would be incomprehensible.

50. *Vorgriff* might be translated as "prior to a grasp," or "pre-apprehension."
51. Rahner, *Hearer of the Word*, 51.
52. David B. Burrell, "Creation or Emanation: Two Paradigms of Reason," in *God and Creation: An Ecumenical Symposium*, ed. David B. Burrell and Bernard McGinn (Notre Dame, Ind.: University of Notre Dame Press, 1990), 28–29.

Chapter 6. **An Alternative Approach**

1. Schleiermacher, *Der christliche Glaube*, rev. ed. (1830/1831), 58, my translation.
2. Rahner, *Foundations*, 63.
3. Ibid., 62.
4. Ibid., 62–63.

5. Robert Sokolowski, "Creation and Christian Understanding," in *God and Creation*, ed. Burrell and McGinn, 191.
6. Ibid., 185.
7. Rahner, *Foundations*, 61.
8. Swinburne describes a miracle as a "divine intervention" which consists in "God temporarily suspending natural laws" (*Is There a God?*, 116).
9. Thiemann, *Revelation and Theology*, 48.
10. Schleiermacher, *The Christian Faith*, 143.
11. Ibid., 142.
12. Ibid., 146–47.
13. Rahner, *Foundations*, 76.
14. Ibid., 77.
15. Ibid., 78.
16. Sokolowski, "Creation and Christian Understanding," 179.
17. Ibid., 191.
18. Ibid., 179.
19. Schleiermacher, *The Christian Faith*, 16.
20. Ibid.
21. Rahner, *Foundations*, 54.
22. Endean, *Karl Rahner and Ignatian Spirituality*, 92. Endean explains that, according to Rahner, God's knowledge of creation is encompassed in the divine self-knowledge. As creatures, we can be in loving contact with this, but the contact is dark and obscure, involving unknowing and surrender.
23. Rahner, *Foundations*, 54.

SELECT BIBLIOGRAPHY

Anselm. *Proslogion*. In *Anselm of Canterbury: The Major Works*, edited by Brian Davies and G. R. Evans. Oxford: Oxford University Press, 1998.

Austin, J. L. *How to Do Things with Words*. Cambridge, Mass.: Harvard University Press, 1962.

———. "Performative Utterances." In *Philosophical Papers*, edited by J. O. Urmson and G. J. Warnock. 2d ed. Oxford: Clarendon Press, 1970.

Ayer, A. J. "Logical Positivism—A Debate." In *A Modern Introduction to Philosophy*, edited by P. Edwards and A. Pap. Rev. ed. New York: The Free Press, 1965.

Barr, James. *The Bible in the Modern World*. New York: Harper and Row, 1973.

Barth, Karl. *Die Theologie und die Kirche*. Zurich, 1928.

Brito, E. *La Pneumatologie de Schleiermacher*. Louvain: Louvain University Press, 1994.

Brunner, Emil. *The Mediator*. London and Redhill: Lutterworth Press, 1934.

———. *Die Mystik und das Wort*. Tübingen: J. C. B. Mohr, 1924.

Buckley, Michael J. *At the Origins of Modern Atheism*. New Haven: Yale University Press, 1987.

Burrell, David B. "Creation or Emanation: Two Paradigms of Reason." In *God and Creation: An Ecumenical Symposium*, edited by David B. Burrell and Bernard McGinn. Notre Dame, Ind.: University of Notre Dame Press, 1990.

Clements, Keith W. *Friedrich Schleiermacher: Pioneer of Modern Theology*. London: Collins, 1987.

Dawkins, Richard. *The Blind Watchmaker*. Harlow, U.K.: Longman Scientific and Technical, 1986.

Elert, Werner. *Der christliche Glaube*. Hamburg: Furche Verlag, 1956.

Endean, Philip. *Karl Rahner and Ignatian Spirituality.* Oxford: Oxford University Press, 2001.
Feuerbach, Ludwig. *Lectures on the Essence of Religion.* New York: Harper and Row, 1967.
———. *Sämtliche Werke.* Vol. 7. *Erläuterungen und Ergänzungen zum Wesen des Christenthums.* Stuttgart–Bad Cannstadt: Günther Holzboog, 1960.
Fischer, Hermann. *Friedrich Schleiermacher.* Munich: Verlag C. H. Beck, 2001.
Frei, Hans. *The Eclipse of Biblical Narrative.* New Haven: Yale University Press, 1975.
Gale, Richard. *On the Nature and Existence of God.* Cambridge: Cambridge University Press, 1991.
Geertz, C. "Religion as a Cultural System." In *The Interpretation of Cultures: Selected Essays,* edited by C. Geertz. New York: Basic Books, 1973.
Geivett, R. Douglas, and Brendan Sweetman, eds. *Contemporary Perspectives on Religious Epistemology.* Oxford: Oxford University Press, 1992.
Gerrish, B. A. *A Prince of the Church: Schleiermacher and the Beginnings of Modern Theology.* London: SCM Press, 1984.
Grayling, A. C., ed. *Philosophy 1: A Guide through the Subject.* New York: Oxford University Press, 1995.
Hauerwas, Stanley. *A Community of Character.* Notre Dame, Ind.: University of Notre Dame Press, 1981.
Hawking, Stephen. *A Brief History of Time.* London: Bantam Press, 1988.
Hegel, G. W. F. *Lectures on the Philosophy of Religion.* Vol. 1. Edited by P. C. Hodgson. Berkeley: University of California Press, 1984.
———. (Foreword). In H. F. W Hinrichs, *Die Religion im inneren Verhältnisse zur Wissenschaft* (Heidelberg, 1822), i–xxviii. German text of 1922 also available as "Hegels *Hinrichs-Vorwort:* Kritische Ausgabe," in *Hegel, Hinrichs, and Schleiermacher on Feeling and Reason in Religion: The Texts of Their 1821–1822 Debate,* appendix, 490–520 (English translation, 245–268). Translated and edited by E. Luft. New York: Edwin Mellen Press, 1987.
Heiler, Friedrich. "The History of Religion as a Preparation for the Cooperation of Religions." In *The History of Religions,* edited by M. Eliade, and J. Kitagawa. Chicago: University of Chicago Press, 1959.
Justin. *The First Apology of Justin.* Kila, Mont.: Kessinger Publishing, 2004.
Kaufman, Gordon. *The Theological Imagination.* Philadelphia: Westminster Press, 1981.
Kelsey, David H. *Uses of Scripture in Recent Theology.* Philadelphia: Fortress Press; London: SCM Press, 1975.
Kerr, Fergus. *Immortal Longings: Versions of Transcending Humanity.* London: SPCK, 1997.
———. *Theology after Wittgenstein.* 2d ed. London: SPCK, 1997.

Kilby, Karen. *Karl Rahner: Theology and Philosophy*. London and New York: Routledge, 2004.
Lamm, Julia A. *The Living God: Schleiermacher's Theological Appropriation of Spinoza*. University Park: Pennsylvania State University Press, 1996.
Lash, Nicholas. *Easter in Ordinary*. London: SCM Press, 1988.
Lindbeck, George A. *The Nature of Doctrine: Religion and Theology in a Postliberal Age*. London: SPCK; Philadelphia: Westminster Press, 1984.
Locke, John. *An Essay Concerning Human Understanding*. Vol. 2. New York: Dover, 1959.
Lonergan, Bernard. *Insight: A Study of Human Understanding*. London: Harper and Row, 1978.
———. *Method in Theology*. London: Darton, Longman and Todd, 1972.
———. *Philosophy of God and Theology*. London: Darton, Longman and Todd, 1973.
Macquarrie, John. *Jesus Christ in Modern Thought*. London: SCM Press, 1990.
Martin, C. B. "A Religious Way of Knowing." In *New Essays in Philosophical Theology*, edited by A. Flew and A. MacIntyre. London: SCM Press, 1955.
Muck, Otto. "Assumptions of a Classical Philosophy of God." *Milltown Studies* 33 (1994): 37–50.
Niebuhr, Richard. *Schleiermacher on Christ and Religion*. London: SCM Press, 1965.
Pannenberg, Wolfhart. *Jesus—God and Man*. Translated by Lewis L. Wilkins and Duane A. Priebe. London: SCM Press, 1968.
Placher, William C. "Postliberal Theology." In *The Modern Theologians: An Introduction to Christian Theology in the Twentieth Century*, edited by David Ford. Rev. ed. Oxford: Blackwell, 1997.
Rahner, Karl. *Foundations of Christian Faith: An Introduction to the Idea of Christianity*. Translated by William V. Dych. New York: Crossroad, 1978; reprint, 1998.
———. *Geist in Welt: Zur Metaphysik der endlichen Erkenntnis bei Thomas von Aquin*. Innsbruck: Rauch, 1939.
———. *Geist in Welt*. In *Sämtliche Werke*, Band 2. Solothurn and Düsseldorf: Benziger; Freiburg: Herder, 1996.
———. *Grundkurs des Glaubens: Einführung in den Begriff des Christentums*. Freiburg: Herder 1984.
———. *Hearer of the Word* (1941). Translated by Joseph Donceel. Edited by Andrew Tallon. New York: Continuum, 1994.
———. *Hörer des Wortes*. In *Sämtliche Werke*, Band 4. Solothurn and Düsseldorf: Benziger; Freiburg: Herder, 1997.
———. *Spirit in the World* (1936). Translated by William V. Dych. London: Sheed and Ward, 1968.

---. *Theological Investigations.* Vol. 4. London: Darton, Longman & Todd, 1966.
Rogers, Kelly, ed. *Self-Interest: An Anthology of Philosophical Perspectives.* London: Routledge, 1997.
Rorty, Richard. *Philosophy and the Mirror of Nature.* Princeton: Princeton University Press, 1979.
Schleiermacher, Friedrich. *The Christian Faith.* 2 vols. Translated and edited by H. R. Mackintosh and J. S. Stewart. New York: Harper and Row, 1963. Reprint with a foreword by B. A. Gerrish, 1 vol., Edinburgh: T & T Clark, 1999.
---. *Der christliche Glaube.* 1st ed. (1821–1822). 2 vols. Edited by Hermann Peiter. Berlin and New York: Walter de Gruyter, 1984.
---. *Der christliche Glaube.* 2d ed. (1830–1831). Edited by Martin Redeker. Berlin and New York: Walter de Gruyter, 1999.
---. *On Religion: Speeches to Its Cultured Despisers.* Translated and edited by Richard Crouter. Cambridge: Cambridge University Press, 1988.
---. *Über die Religion: Reden an die Gebildeten unter ihren Varächten.* Stuttgart: Reclam, 1969.
Sokolowski, Robert. "Creation and Christian Understanding." In *God and Creation: An Ecumenical Symposium,* edited by David B. Burrell and Bernard McGinn. Notre Dame, Ind.: University of Notre Dame Press, 1990.
Swinburne, R. *The Coherence of Theism.* Oxford: Clarendon Press, 1977, 1993.
---. *The Existence of God.* Oxford: Clarendon Press, 1979; rev. ed., 1991.
---. *Faith and Reason.* Oxford: Clarendon Press, 1981; rev. ed., 2005.
---. "Intellectual Biography." In *Reason and the Christian Religion: Essays in Honour of Richard Swinburne,* edited by Alan G. Padgett. Oxford: Clarendon Press, 1994.
---. *Is There a God?* Oxford: Oxford University Press, 1996.
Taliaferro, C. *Contemporary Philosophy of Religion.* Oxford: Blackwell, 1998.
Thiemann, Ronald F. *Revelation and Theology: The Gospel as Narrated Promise.* Notre Dame, Ind.: University of Notre Dame Press, 1985.
Thomas Aquinas. *Summa contra Gentiles.* Vol. 1. Translated by A. C. Pegis. New York: Image Books, 1955.
---. *Summa Theologiae.* Vol. 2. Edited by T. McDermott. London: Blackfriars, 1964.
---. *Summa Theologiae.* Vol. 3. Edited by Herbert McCabe. London: Blackfriars, 1964.
---. *Summa Theologiae.* Vol. 12. Translated by P. T. Durbin. London: Blackfriars, 1968.
Torrance, Thomas. *Reality and Evangelical Theology.* Philadelphia: Westminster Press, 1982.
---. *Theological Science.* Oxford: Oxford University Press, 1969.

Vass, George. *A Theologian in Search of a Philosophy: Understanding Karl Rahner.* Vol. 1. London: Sheed and Ward, 1985.
Williams, R. "Schleiermacher and Feuerbach on the Intentionality of Religious Consciousness." *The Journal of Religion* 53 (1973): 424–55.
Wingren, Gustaf. *Theology in Conflict.* Philadelphia: Muhlenberg, 1958.
Wood, Charles. *The Formation of Christian Understanding: An Essay in Theological Hermeneutics.* Philadelphia: Westminster Press, 1981.

INDEX

Alston, William, 20
analytic philosophy, 5–6, 39
Anselm of Canterbury
  on *fides quarens intellectum,* 16
  ontological argument, 16, 22, 131–32, 152
Aristotle, 11, 121
Augustine, St., 131
Austin, J. L., 6, 7
  on locutionary vs. illocutionary acts, 78, 83
  on performative utterances, 41, 44, 160nn.21, 23
Ayer, A. J., 5, 157n.6

Barr, James, 74–75
Barth, Karl
  Rahner on, 62
  and Schleiermacher, 90, 165n.8
  and Thiemann, 36, 50, 51, 56–57, 153, 162n.8
Bayes's theorem, 19, 21
Brito, E., 167n.43
Brunner, Emil
  Der Mittler, 90
  Die Mystik und das Wort, 89–90
  Rahner on, 62

  on Schleiermacher, 89–90, 165n.8
Buckley, Michael J.
  At the Origins of Modern Atheism, 2, 87–88
  on Schleiermacher, 103–4, 105, 109–10
Bultmann, Rudolf, 160n.6
Burrell, David, 137

Calvinism, 50
Catholicism, 4, 30, 72
Clements, Keith W., 166n.29
contingency and perfection, 23–24
cosmological argument, 17, 132, 152
Council of Trent: *De justificatione,* 30
creation
  creatio continua/continuous preservation, 65, 143–45
  and human freedom, 147–49
  Rahner on, 143, 145–46, 172n.22
Crouter, Richard, 101–2, 165n.2

Darwin, Charles, 14–15
Dawkins, Richard, 11, 12

179

deductive arguments, 16–17, 22–23, 112–13
deism, 87
Descartes, René, 87, 170n.16
Dewey, John: on warranted assertability, 74
Donceel, Joseph, 169n.2, 171n.40

efficient causality, 87–88
Elert, Werner, 50
Endean, Philip: on Rahner, 124, 149, 170n.39, 171n.40, 172n.22
end of the world, 76–77
Enlightenment, the: insistence on evidence during, 1, 2, 35, 49
Eucharistic Prayer, 78–79
evidence for belief
    Enlightenment insistence on, 1, 2, 35–36, 49
    and logical positivism, 5–7, 157n.6
    and Rahner, 130–33, 135–36, 151–54, 155
    and Schleiermacher, 98, 103, 108–10, 111–15, 133, 151–54, 155
    and Swinburne, 3–4, 16–24, 28, 30–33, 153–54
    and Thiemann, 36, 50, 52, 72, 73–82, 84, 153
    See also foundationalism; intuition
evolutionary theory: natural selection, 14–15

faith
    Anselm on, 16
    relationship to reason, 11, 30–31, 35, 48, 52–53, 56–62, 63–65, 67, 84, 135, 137–38, 140, 153, 162n.28
    relationship to self-interest/self-denial, 28–30
    relationship to trust/action, 25–26, 28–30, 38
    Swinburne on, 24–30, 89
    truths of reason vs. truths of, 11, 30–31, 35, 48, 52–53, 60–61, 67
    See also revelation
Feuerbach, Ludwig, 104, 167n.43
Fichte, Johann Gottlieb
    on morality, 93
    on principle of identity, 101
    and Schleiermacher, 91–93, 101
    Science of Knowledge, 91–92, 101
Fischer, Hermann, 166n.13
foundationalism
    defined, 36–37, 52, 61, 63, 64
    Lindbeck on, 36–37, 48
    and Rahner, 133–38
    relationship to language, 64
    relationship to philosophy, 133–34, 156
    Rorty on, 55–56
    Thiemann on, 36–37, 51–53, 55–56, 59, 60–62, 63–65, 67, 70, 74, 75, 77, 81, 82, 84, 85, 89, 98–99, 120, 133, 134, 162n.28
Fourth Lateran Council, 9
Frei, Hans, 36, 37, 69, 163n.49
Friedrich, Casper David
    "Monk by the Sea," 90–91
    "Winter Landscape," 90–91

Gerrish, B. A., 165n.6
God
    as creator, 2, 4, 9, 23, 65, 142–49, 150, 153, 154, 155, 172n.22
    defined, 4–5
    essence of, 22
    eternity of, 4, 9
    as Father, 90
    as first cause of existence, 2, 12, 87–88, 147, 150, 153, 154–56

freedom of, 4
goodness of, 4, 7–8, 10, 42–43
grace of, 50, 51, 56–57, 66–67, 110, 111, 118, 119, 137, 143, 150, 153, 154, 155
as ground of human knowledge, 10, 31–32, 33, 118–19, 129–33, 135–36, 142–43, 145–46, 148–56, 171n.39
hiddenness of, 76–77
identification of, 73, 75–76, 77, 78–81, 82
incorporeality of, 9
infinity of, 9, 31, 33, 35–36, 52, 88–89, 93–94, 117, 118–19, 128, 129–30, 150–51, 154
knowledge of, 1–2, 16–24, 31–32, 35–36, 48, 50, 51–53, 58–59, 88–89, 99, 117, 118–19, 120–25, 126–33, 134, 150–56
and language, 124–27, 132, 135–38, 154
and miracles, 143, 172n.8
omnipotence of, 14–15
perfection of, 4, 9–10, 42–43
as permanent accompaniment to all human experience, 88, 107–8, 113, 117, 129–33, 142–43
primary vs. secondary beliefs regarding, 4–5
priority of, 28, 50, 51–52, 66–67, 74–75, 80–81
promises of, 73, 75, 77–83
relationship to human nature, 61–62
Scripture and agency of, 76–77
simplicity of, 9
as spirit, 4
trustworthiness of, 28–29, 77–81, 82
wisdom of, 7–8

God's existence
C-inductive arguments for, 18, 19, 20–21
as explaining order of universe, 12–14, 19
as explaining souls joined to bodies, 14–16
as "God of the gaps" postulate, 13–14
ontological argument for, 16, 22, 131–32, 152
P-inductive arguments for, 17–18, 19, 20–21
probability of, 3–4, 16–24, 28, 33
Rahner on, 115, 118, 130–33, 137, 151, 152–53, 155
Schleiermacher on, 103, 108–10, 111–15, 130, 133, 151, 152–53, 155
Swinburne on, 3–4, 16–24, 28, 33, 49–50
Thomas Aquinas's Five Ways, 11, 16
God's transcendence
and creation, 142–47
and God as first cause of existence, 2, 87–88, 150, 153, 154–56
vs. God's immanence, 140–41, 142–46
and Lindbeck, 1–2, 36, 48
and Rahner, 117, 119, 123–24, 128, 139, 140–41, 142–43, 150–51, 153, 154, 155–56
and Schleiermacher, 93–94, 98, 112–13, 117, 119, 139, 140, 142–44, 150–51, 153
and Swinburne, 1–2, 4, 10, 15–16, 24, 31, 32–33, 88–89, 139, 143, 150
and Thiemann, 1–2, 36, 50, 52, 56, 63, 64, 68, 88–89, 139–40, 143, 150
Gutting, Gary, 20

Hauerwas, Stanley, 36, 37
  on revelation, 50–51
Hawking, Stephen, 11, 12
Hegel, G. W. F., 91–92, 166n.37
  on Schleiermacher, 102–3, 104, 167nn.43, 44
Heiler, Friedrich, 47
Hick, John, 20
Hinrich, H. F. W.: *Die Religion im inneren Verhältnisse zur Wissenschaft*, 103
human freedom, 33, 154, 155
  Lindbeck on, 147
  Rahner on, 148–49
  relationship to creation, 147–49
  relationship to human nescience, 17, 25, 147
  Schleiermacher on, 100, 106–7, 127–28, 139, 147, 148
  Swinburne on, 2, 17, 25, 32, 66, 67, 147
  Thiemann on, 2, 65–67, 140, 147
human perfection, 9, 10
human transcendence: Rahner on, 118–19, 123–24, 126–27, 129–33, 135–36, 139, 142–43, 145–46, 148–49, 151, 152–53, 155–56, 171n.39
Hume, David, 103

inductive arguments, 3–4, 16, 17–24
intuition
  Kant on, 101–2
  Rahner on, 64, 120–21, 124, 128
  Schleiermacher on, 98–102
  Thiemann on, 52, 56, 59, 61, 63–66, 67, 83–84, 98–99, 102, 106, 143, 162n.20
  See also foundationalism
Islam, 4, 5
  Mohammed the Prophet, 27
Israel, people of, 76, 79

Jacobi, F. H., 103
Jesus Christ
  God's self-revelation in, 31, 32–33, 44, 52, 76, 79, 81, 119, 126–27, 153, 155
  as Incarnation, 4, 28, 90, 141–42, 153, 155
  as Lord, 27
  and the Mass, 4
  resurrection of, 77, 79, 80, 83
  as Savior/Redeemer, 30, 97–98, 110, 111, 126–27, 150
Judaism, 4, 5
Justin Martyr, 35, 159n.1

Kant, Immanuel, 59, 75
  on existence, 22
  on God, 44–45, 92
  on intuition (*Anschauung*), 101–2
  on practical reason, 92, 93–94, 100, 101–2
  on transcendental knowledge, 118, 166n.13
Kelsey, David, 68, 69, 71
Kepler, Johannes, 13
Kerr, Fergus, 122, 123, 169n.13
Kierkegaard, Søren, 56–57, 58, 61, 84, 162n.28
Kilby, Karen, 133–35
knowledge
  causal model of, 55–60, 61, 64–68, 140
  of God, 1–2, 16–24, 31–32, 35–36, 48, 50, 51–53, 58–59, 88–89, 99, 117, 118–19, 120–25, 126–33, 134, 150–56
  God as ground of, 10, 31–32, 33, 129–33, 135–36, 142–43, 145–46, 148–56, 171n.39
  as mediated by finite reality, 1, 2, 18–19, 33, 36, 49, 52, 88–89,

98–102, 117, 120–21, 125, 126–27, 134, 150–51, 154–56
and sight metaphors, 67
Thiemann on normal means of knowing, 61, 63–66, 83
See also foundationalism; revelation; truth

Lamm, Julia, 105, 107–8, 168n.48
language
  Rahner on the word "God," 125–27, 132, 135–38, 154
  relationship to foundationalism, 64
  Wittgenstein on, 69, 70, 114, 123, 124, 169n.16
Lash, Nicholas: *Easter in Ordinary*, 114
Leibniz, Gottfried Wilhelm, 132
Lessing, Gotthold Ephraim, 87
Lindbeck, George
  on conformity of self to God, 40, 41–42
  and ecumenism, 37, 45–46, 160n.5
  on ethics and religious language, 40
  on experiential-expressivist approach to revelation, 37, 39, 40, 44–48, 53, 160n.6
  on foundationalism, 36–37, 48
  and God's transcendence, 1–2, 36, 48
  on human freedom, 147
  on justification of faith, 1, 36
  on Kant, 44–45, 160n.6
  on Lonergan, 40, 46–48
  The Nature of Doctrine, 36, 160n.5
  on performative utterances, 41, 44, 160n.23
  on Rahner, 48, 160n.6
  on rationalist/propositional approach to revelation, 37–44, 48, 160n.6
  on regulative function of Christian doctrine, 37–38, 39–41, 44, 45, 47, 48, 69, 72
  on Schleiermacher, 45, 47, 53, 160n.6
  vs. Swinburne, 1–2, 38–39, 40, 48, 147
  vs. Thiemann, 1–2, 36–37, 38, 49, 50, 53, 69, 72, 73, 147
  on Thomas Aquinas, 42–43, 160n.6
  on truth, 37–44, 48
Locke, John, 60–61
logical positivism, 5–7, 157n.6
Lonergan, Bernard, 40, 160n.6
  Method in Theology, 46–47
  on religious experience, 46–48
Lutheranism, 36, 48, 50, 51, 78, 139, 153, 162n.8

Macquarrie, John, 167n.43
Maréchal, Joseph, 118
Martin, C. B., 19–20
Matthew, Gospel of, 79, 83
Melanchthon, Philipp, 77
Mersenne, Marin, 87
Metz, Johannes Baptist, 168n.2
Muck, Otto, 22–24

Newton, Isaac, 13
Nicene Creed, 26–27
Niebuhr, Richard, 165n.8

ontological argument, 16, 22, 131–32, 152
ordinary-language philosophy, 6–7
Otto, Rudolf, 160n.6

Pannenberg, Wolfhart, 76–77
pantheism, 140–41, 168n.48

Paul, St.
    1 Cor. 15.26, 111
    1 Cor. 15.55, 111
Peirce, Charles, 63
perfection
    and contingency, 23–24
    in creatures, 9, 10, 43
    of God, 4, 9–10, 42–43
performative utterances, 41, 44, 71
Phillips, D. Z., 29
philosophy
    analytic philosophy, 5–6, 39
    ordinary-language philosophy, 6–7
    relationship to foundationalism, 133–34, 156
    relationship to theology, 133–38, 156
Plato, 11
postmodernism, 49
predestination, 66–67
Protestantism, 4, 30, 77, 110, 112, 165n.2
    Evangelical Church of Prussian Union, 103, 111
    Lutheranism, 36, 48, 50, 51, 78, 139, 153, 162n.8
    Rahner on theology in, 61–62
    Thiemann on theology in, 37, 50–53, 56–60, 63–64, 67, 71–72, 73, 162n.8

Rahner, Karl
    on Barth, 62
    on Brunner, 62
    on creation, 143, 145–46, 172n.22
    Endean on, 124, 149, 170n.39, 171n.40, 172n.22
    and foundationalism, 133–38
    on *Gegenstand* vs. *Objekt*, 170n.39
    Geist in Welt/Spirit in the World, 64, 117, 118, 120–21, 124, 128–29, 169n.8
    on God as infinite horizon of human transcendence/ground of human knowledge, 118–19, 129–33, 135–36, 142–43, 145–46, 148–49, 151–54, 155–56, 171n.39
    on God's existence, 115, 118, 130–33, 137, 151, 152–53, 155
    on God's grace, 118, 119, 143, 150
    and God's transcendence, 117, 119, 123–24, 128, 139, 140–41, 142–43, 150–51, 153, 154, 155–56
    Grundkurs des Glaubens/Foundations of Christian Faith, 118, 123, 129, 132, 171n.39
    Hörer des Wortes/Hearer of the Word, 61–62, 117–18, 121–22, 126–27, 131, 132, 136, 168n.2, 171n.40
    on human freedom, 148–49
    on human historicity, 126–27, 134
    on human nature, 61–62
    on human transcendence, 118–19, 123–24, 126–27, 129–33, 135–36, 139, 142–43, 145–46, 148–49, 151, 152–53, 155–56, 171n.39
    on intuition, 64, 120–21, 124, 128
    on Jesus Christ, 119, 126–27
    Kerr on, 122, 123
    on Kierkegaard, 62
    Kilby on, 133–34
    on knowledge of God, 120–25, 126–33, 134, 135–36, 150–51, 169n.13
    Lindbeck on, 48, 160n.6
    on pantheism, 140–41

on Protestant theologians, 61–62
on reason and faith, 61–62
relationship between philosophy and theology in, 133–38
on revelation, 61–62, 118, 119, 126–27, 134, 135, 143
on Ritschl, 62
on salvation, 126–27
vs. Schleiermacher, 2, 62, 89, 91, 94, 115, 117, 119, 130, 133–34, 139–41, 142–46, 148, 150–53, 154, 155–56
on science, 121–22
vs. Thiemann, 61–62, 120
and Thomas Aquinas, 91, 117, 118–19, 120–21, 128–29
on unthematic self-consciousness, 123, 135–36
on *Vorgriff,* 131–32, 135–36, 171n.50
on the word "God," 125–27, 132, 135–38, 150, 151, 154
reason
Lindbeck on rationalist/propositional approach to revelation, 37–44, 48, 160n.6
relationship to faith/revelation, 11, 30–31, 35, 48, 52–53, 56–62, 63–65, 67, 84, 135, 137–38, 140, 153, 162n.28
Swinburne's rationalism, 2, 3–4, 5–6, 10, 17, 24–33, 35–36, 38–39, 49–50, 153–54
Thomas Aquinas on, 11, 30–31
Torrance on, 57–60
truths of faith vs. truths of, 11, 30–31, 35, 48, 52–53, 60–61, 67
revelation
dialectical approach to, 53
Erlert on, 50

of God in Christ, 31, 32–33, 44, 52, 76, 79, 81, 119, 126–27, 153, 155
Hauerwas on, 50–51
Lindbeck on experiential-expressivist approach to, 37, 39, 40, 44–48, 53, 160n.6
Lindbeck on rationalist/propositional approach to, 37–44, 48, 160n.6
Rahner on, 61–62
relationship to Christian community, 74–75, 78, 79
relationship to reason, 35, 53, 56–62, 63–65, 84, 135, 137–38, 140, 153, 162n.28
Schleiermacher on, 53–55, 98–99, 108–10, 111, 119
Thiemann on, 1, 36, 50–73, 75–77, 78–83, 110, 153
Thomas Aquinas on, 11, 30–31
Torrance on, 57–60, 65–66
See also faith
Richard, Michael, 168n.2
Ricoeur, Paul, 83
Ritschl, Albrecht, 62
Romanticism, 90–91, 105
Rorty, Richard: on foundationalism, 55–56

salvation, 28, 29–30, 66–67, 95–98, 126–27, 159n.61
Schleiermacher, Friedrich
Brunner on, 89–90, 165n.8
Buckley on, 103–4
The Christian Faith, 53–54, 93, 94, 95–96, 103, 105–6, 109, 111, 113, 166n.13
on creation, 142–45, 146
on dogmatic propositions, 93, 111
on ethics, 92, 94, 99, 100

Schleiermacher, Friedrich (*cont.*)
  on feeling of absolute
    dependence, 54–55, 62, 93,
    94–95, 98, 99–100, 101–7,
    108–10, 112–13, 114–15, 119,
    127–28, 130, 133, 139, 142–44,
    147, 151, 152–53, 165n.8
  vs. Feuerbach, 104
  and Fichte, 91–93, 101
  on God as permanent
    accompaniment to all human
    experience, 107–8, 113, 117,
    127–28
  on God's existence, 103, 108–10,
    111–15, 130, 133, 151, 152–53,
    155
  on God's grace, 111
  and God's transcendence, 93–94,
    98, 112–13, 117, 119, 139, 140,
    142–44, 150–51, 153
  Hegel on, 102–3, 104, 167nn.43, 44
  on human freedom, 100, 106–7,
    127–28, 139, 147, 148
  on immediate self-consciousness,
    54–55
  on intuition, 98–102, 166n.32
  on Jesus Christ, 97–98, 110, 111,
    150
  vs. Kant, 92, 93–94, 100, 101–2,
    166n.13
  Lamm on, 105, 107–8, 168n.48
  Lash on, 114
  Lindbeck on, 45, 47, 53, 160n.6
  *On Religion: Speeches to Its
    Cultured Despisers*, 89, 94,
    99–100, 104–5, 111, 165n.2
  on pantheism, 140, 168n.48
  on piety (*Frömmigkeit*), 91,
    94–100, 101–10, 111, 114–15,
    127–28, 152, 154
  vs. Rahner, 2, 89, 91, 94, 115, 117,
    119, 130, 133–34, 139–41,
    142–46, 148, 150–53, 154,
    155–56
  on redemption (*Erlösung*), 95–98,
    110, 119, 150
  on revelation, 53–55, 98–99,
    108–10, 111, 119
  and Romanticism, 90–91, 105
  on Scripture, 111–12
  on subjective idealism, 91–92,
    168n.48
  Thiemann on, 53–55, 61, 98–99,
    102, 106–7, 109, 110, 133
  on transcendental
    theology/philosophy, 91–94,
    99, 100, 111
  use of term "God" by, 113–15,
    131, 150, 151, 154
Scholasticism, 14, 23–24, 35, 42,
  87–88, 131, 146, 170n.39
science, 171n.49
  quantum theory, 7, 8
  relativity theory, 7, 8
  Swinburne on, 6–7, 8–9, 10–16,
    24, 39
Scripture
  authority of, 69, 70, 71, 72–73
  interpretation of, 70, 80–81,
    84–85
  Kelsey on, 68, 69, 71
  as narrative whole, 69–70, 71–73,
    75–76, 79–82, 163n.49
  relationship to God's
    trustworthiness, 78
  relationship to recognition by
    readers, 81–85
  Schleiermacher on, 111–12
  Thiemann on, 68–73, 75–77,
    78–81, 84–85
  and Thomas Aquinas, 23
  Wood on, 68, 69–71, 82
self-interest, 28–30, 31
Sokolowski, Robert, 141–42, 146–47

soul and body, 14–16
Swinburne, Richard
  on analogous statements, 7–9
  and analytic philosophy, 5–6, 39
  on Christian faith, 24–30, 89
  The Coherence of Theism, 3, 4–5
  on definition of theism, 4–5
  on evidence for belief, 3–4, 16–24, 28, 30–33
  The Existence of God, 3, 10, 16–19, 21
  Faith and Reason, 3, 5, 25, 159n.61
  and God's transcendence, 1–2, 4, 10, 15–16, 24, 31, 32–33, 88–89, 139, 143, 150
  on human freedom, 2, 17, 25, 32, 66, 67, 147
  "Intellectual Biography," 7, 13
  Is There a God?, 10–11
  vs. Lindbeck, 1–2, 38–39, 40, 48, 147
  on meaningfulness/coherence of theism, 3, 4–10
  on metaphysics, 3, 6, 12–24, 31
  on miracles, 143, 172n.8
  on Nicene Creed, 26–27
  on principle of credulity, 19, 20–21
  on probability of Christian beliefs, 1, 3, 4, 25–30, 33, 38–39, 78
  on probability of God's existence, 3–4, 16–24, 28, 33, 49–50
  rationalism of, 2, 3–4, 5–6, 10, 17, 24–33, 35–36, 38–39, 49–50, 153–54
  on religious experience, 16, 18–21, 25, 27, 29, 31–32
  on salvation, 28, 29–30, 159n.61
  on science, 6–7, 8–9, 10–16, 24, 39
  vs. Thiemann, 1–2, 49–50, 66, 67, 78, 88–89, 150, 153–54
  on Thomas Aquinas, 7–8, 11, 14
  on trust in God, 25–26, 28–30, 38

Tallon, Andrew, 169n.2
Thiemann, Ronald
  and Barth, 36, 50, 51, 56–57, 153, 162n.8
  on causal model of revelation, 55–60, 61, 64–68, 140
  on creation, 143
  on Eucharistic Prayer, 78–79
  on foundationalism, 36–37, 51–53, 55–56, 59, 60–62, 63–65, 67, 70, 74, 75, 77, 81, 82, 84, 85, 89, 98–99, 120, 133, 134, 162n.28
  on functionalism, 68–74
  on God's hiddenness, 76–77
  on God's prevenience, 50, 51–52, 53, 56–57, 65, 72, 73, 75, 76, 78–79, 80, 82–84, 109, 162n.8
  on God's promises, 73, 75, 77–83, 84–85
  and God's transcendence, 1–2, 36, 50, 52, 56, 63, 64, 68, 88–89, 139–40, 143, 150
  on God's trustworthiness, 77–81, 82
  on human freedom, 2, 65–67, 140, 147
  on illocutionary acts, 78–79, 80–81, 82, 85
  on interlocutionary acts, 83, 85
  on intuition, 52, 56, 59, 61, 63–66, 67, 83–84, 98–99, 102, 106, 143, 162n.20
  on justification of Christian belief, 36, 72, 73–82, 84, 153
  vs. Lindbeck, 1–2, 36–37, 38, 49, 50, 53, 69, 72, 73, 147
  on Locke, 60–61

Thiemann, Ronald (*cont.*)
  on locutionary acts, 78–79, 80–81, 82, 85
  on normal means of knowing, 61, 63–66, 83
  on Protestant theologians, 37, 50–53, 56–60, 63–64, 67, 71–72, 73, 162n.8
  vs. Rahner, 61–62, 120
  on reason, 52–53, 56–60, 63
  on recognition, 81–85
  on revelation, 1, 36, 50–73, 75–77, 78–83, 110, 153
  Revelation and Theology, 36, 50
  on Schleiermacher, 53–55, 61, 98–99, 102, 106–7, 109, 110, 133
  on Scripture, 68–73, 75–77, 78–81, 84–85
  vs. Swinburne, 1–2, 49–50, 66, 67, 78, 88–89, 150, 153–54
  on Torrance, 57–60, 61, 65–66, 84, 162nn.20, 28
Thomas Aquinas
  on analogous terms, 7, 8–9, 42–43
  and Aristotle, 11
  on creation *ex nihilo*, 23
  on *excessus*, 128–29
  Five Ways, 11, 16
  on God, 7–8, 9–10, 11, 22–23, 42–43, 154
  on intelligible species, 120, 169nn.7, 8
  on knowledge of the metaphysical, 120–21
  Lindbeck on, 42–43, 160n.6
  on principle that everything moved is moved by another, 22–23
  and Rahner, 91, 117, 118–19, 120–21, 128–29
  on reason, 11, 30–31
  on revelation, 11, 30–31
  and Scripture, 23
  Summa contra Gentiles, 11
  Summa Theologiae, 11, 23, 43, 117, 120
  Swinburne on, 7–8, 11, 14
  on truth as correspondence, 42
  on truths of faith, 30–31
  on univocal predication, 7–8, 9–10
Tillich, Paul, 160n.6
Torrance, Thomas, 57–60, 61, 65–66, 84, 162nn.20, 28
Trinity, the, 11, 35, 79
truth
  Lindbeck on, 37–44, 48
  relationship to coherence, 40, 63, 64, 74, 81–82, 84
  relationship to correspondence, 40, 41–44, 64–65, 73
  truths of faith vs. truths of reason, 11, 30–31, 35, 48, 52–53, 60–61, 67
  and warranted assertability, 74, 77
  See also knowledge

Wainwright, William, 20
warranted assertability, 74, 77
Williams, R., 167n.43
Wingren, Gustaf, 51, 161n.2
Wittgenstein, Ludwig, 69, 70, 114, 123, 124, 169n.16
Wood, Charles, 68, 69–70, 71, 82, 163nn.49, 51

Yandell, Keith, 20

ANNE E. INMAN

is an adjunct associate professor at the University of Notre Dame, London Centre, and a lecturer at Birkbeck College, University of London, and the University of Roehampton.

www.ingramcontent.com/pod-product-compliance
Lightning Source LLC
Chambersburg PA
CBHW070402240426
43661CB00056B/2500